The Language of Brands

of Brands

A Linguistic Framework for
Creating Brand Distinction

ROBERT BAILEY

www.rawbailey.com

Cataloging-in-Publication Data
Names: Bailey, Robert author.
Title: The Language of Brands:
A Linguistic Framework for Creating Brand Distinction
Description First Edition. | Rawcon Press.
Identifiers: ISBN 9781661927189 (Paperback) ASIN 1659765633 (ebook)
Subjects: Linguistics, Marketing
Printed in the United States of America

ISBN 9781661927189

"Control over discourse and its properties are forms of the direct enactment of social or institutional power"

- Teun A. van Dijk

For Bella,
Who taught me the
true value of language.

Contents

Introduction

A History of Branding

1. Why Language?   3

2. The Coca Cola Shift   14

How We Perceive Brand

3. How Does Language Work?   28

4. The Origin of Meaning   38

5. Creating a Story   49

6. The Feature Fallacy   59

Shift

Introduction   73

7. Picking Apart Language   77

8. Language and Brand   92

9. Understanding Your Industry's Language   108

10. Understanding Your Audience's Language   132

11. Driving Shift   156

12. Measuring Shift   173

13. Conclusion   178

Acknowledgements   182

Notes   185

Diagrams

About the Author   203

Index   204

Introduction

There's a new rule in marketing: brands must speak to consumers using their language.

No longer is it enough to use simple data analysis and smart creative to draw in audiences. In a modern, competitive landscape, marketers now have to think about how they can truly connect with consumers. And it's through a foundation of trust, resonance, and relatability that these connections are built.

Unfortunately, traditional methods for understanding consumers only provide a snapshot of the challenges that brands face. Persona, competitor, and market research; A/B and user testing; campaign and content frameworks; and data analysis are all only smaller pieces of a much larger puzzle. Individually, they all offer limited insights, and when brought together, they often create a disconnected and unbalanced marketing narrative. At best, this means inconsistent campaigns. At worst, it means failure.

Overcoming these problems means understanding how to connect with consumers on their turf, in their language, and concerning topics they care about. It means building a stronger, balanced marketing and analytics effort that takes into account traditional marketing tools and analytics, but also considers the role of an in-depth, holistic framework for continued iteration. In simple terms, it means building a brand through language.

But the separate concepts of language and brand are almost as difficult to pinpoint as one another. What makes language a tool for distinction, and how can it be controlled? What exactly constitutes a brand, and is it possible for a brand's marketing efforts to ever stand separate from the brand itself?

That is what The Language of Brands is about. As easy as it would be to simplify language as an agreed-upon mechanism for communication, and brand as an agreed-upon way in which a company is perceived, the reality is far more complex. This book explores how it is complex and why taking steps towards integrating language into your branding efforts can uncover strategies you otherwise may not have considered. While it does this, it explores the nature of language as a part of the marketing machine and provides a clear psychological framework for how consumers receive and digest brands through language.

After all, language has a place in almost every facet of our lives. From the words we write on our computer screens to the images and signs we digest every waking moment—and the processes that take place inside our heads to understand these experiences.

So, as something that pervades everything we do, language's role in marketing and branding should not be surprising. As we'll uncover throughout this book, its role is more than just analysis. This is especially true in a world where search algorithms have come to decide what audiences see. Every touchpoint now needs to not only resonate with human audiences but with machine learning systems as well.

Google Search and Facebook content delivery are excellent examples. Both of these tools, used by consumers daily, are based on linguistic factors that have been turned into algorithms for measuring potential interest. Both analyze the language of digital touchpoints to measure the degree to which content will resonate with users. They then deliver what they believe to be relevant content to users.

In a race to maintain their visibility, businesses have continued to develop processes for the delivery of the best and most relevant content, using natural language processing to better understand what individuals are looking for and how to define it. Even paid social ads leverage linguistic indicators to chart the fine line between spam and relevancy.

As a result, linguists are increasingly relevant in the areas of branding, persona identification, Search Engine Optimization (SEO), social media marketing, ad creation, and content strategy. Their ability to channel language in both data-backed and creative projects provides them with the ability to create content that resonates with both machines and people.

And it's not just these areas that show a need for language experts. All aspects of content and brand creation and curation provide a properly trained linguist with the opportunity to leverage a combination of data and creativity to optimize content for clicks, engagement, conversion, and advocacy.

This is where Shift comes in. As the main strategy being discussed, Shift considers language to be the product of social and discourse conventions. As such, it positions language as a vehicle for brand change and growth. In brief, Shift is a linguistic approach designed to influence and 'shift' social and discourse conventions surrounding a brand from one position to another by carefully manipulating language, tone, and style. In doing this, it pays attention to the wealth of scientific material and methods available to the modern marketer, while also providing a rationale for the creation of campaigns that consider more than just traditional marketing techniques

For almost ten years, I've worked with language, semiotics, and marketing to create, test, and iterate on various linguistic-based strategies. I've worked with a huge array of different marketing problems, and I've come up with solutions that help marketers to get there faster, without any of the padded fluff you often see.

This book aims to provide an introduction to how linguistics can and should be a piece of the marketing puzzle, as well as a brief but detailed guide on how non-linguist marketers can implement linguistics in the areas of branding, persona identification, social media, SEO, content strategy, and *Shift* effectively.

Part 1

A History of Branding

*If I'd asked customers what they wanted,
they would have told me, 'A faster
horse!'*

- Henry Ford

1

Why Language?

In the westernmost district of Pompeii lies the ruins of what was, during the 1st century AD, one of the city's most opulent residences. The home exemplified the lavishness of the Pompeii elite, standing three stories tall and situated on a prime piece of real estate. From the entrance, you would have been able to smell the breeze of the coast, hear the bustle of the forum, and see the roof of the basilica. Rich flora would have been draped over the walls, with luxurious goods adorning each of the rooms inside. A private bathroom, particularly rare in those times, could be found by walking through any one of the three atriums that guarded the entrance to the building.

But this home isn't significant because of its location or its opulence. While impressive, it is what we find in one of the atriums that, as linguistic marketers, sparks our curiosity. There, still standing today—and having survived the eruption of Mount Vesuvius—lies a mosaic, one depicting four large fish sauce vessels, each with its own inscription: [1]

Gari Flos Scom Scauri, Ex Offici, Na Scau, Ri
The flower of garum, made of the mackerel, a product of Scaurus, from the shop of Scaurus

Liquuminis Flos
The flower of Liquamen

Gari Flos Scombri
The flower of garum, made of the mackerel

Liquamen Optimum Ex Officin A Scauri
The best liquamen, from the shop of Scaurus

If you had been born in the 1st century AD, all it would have taken would have been one look for you to know whose home you were in. The inscription "Gari Flos" (the flower of garum) was a familiar slogan throughout the Mediterranean. Just like the modern slogans "Just Do It" from Nike and "Finger Lickin' Good" from KFC, "Gari Flos" was indicative of a particular product and brand. In this case, a type of fish sauce called garum, manufactured by one of Pompeii's elite: Umbricius Scaurus. [2]

Not much is known about Scaurus. Many of the records that described his life were lost when Mount Vesuvius erupted. What we do know, however, is that it is likely Scaurus was a man who made his fortune, as opposed to inheriting it. We also know that he amassed a lot of it through the production and sale of garum. Never shy of his own success, his lavish home meant little when compared to the bottles of it he sent around the world, all also branded with the slogans above.

It's said that Scaurus would spend his evenings standing on the third floor of his residence, looking towards the coast and watching as ships sailed away carrying his products. And with good reason; his particular brand of garum became very popular throughout the known world, providing added taste to otherwise bland meals. By the time of his death, his fish sauce had become so popular that bottles had traveled as far as the south of France—an incredible distance at the time.

But what made Scaurus's fish sauce so popular wasn't just the taste. As Gallic nobility imported his products to enjoy with their meals, they thought of more than just the physical attributes of the sauce.

To understand the reason why Scaurus's fish sauce became so popular, we must first consider what garum actually is. Made by crushing the intestines of fish, garum is a type of fermented fish sauce that was popular in ancient Greece, Rome, Carthage, and Byzantium. While the finished product is often very mild, a byproduct of the production process is an incredibly unpleasant smell. So unpleasant, in fact, that factories were often required to exist on the outskirts of cities. As a result, the only contact many Romans would have with the fish sauce would have been with the final product, which, while mild, still brought with it the smell of raw fish—an ultimately unpleasant smell.

So when Scaurus used a simple metaphor—the flower of—to brand his fish sauce, he challenged commonly held opinions of fish sauce. Simply put, the smell of flowers contradicted the smell of fish sauce: one smells nice, the other smells bad. It was because of this metaphor that it didn't matter if someone had tried his product. The language that was used to describe it— like a flower—changed customer expectations. In other words, the rhetoric used was powerful enough to override common-sense knowledge that fish sauce smells like fish. Whether knowingly or not, Scaurus marketed his product through language.

At first, this may seem nonsensical. Consumers know better, right? However, lots of modern brands do this. Think of fast food restaurants, which brand their food as healthy and nutritionally valuable even though we know it's not. Or consider sports apparel brands that associate their products with athletic success, when the reality is that they have little bearing on an individual's ability. It is language that lies at the heart of all these marketing campaigns and essentially turns one thing into another.

While Scaurus is sometimes lauded as being one of the first marketers, what he did wasn't entirely unique. Language has been a marketing tool for as long as selling and trading have existed. At the center of exchanges, rhetoric has often found itself prized above all else, with the "gift of the gab" being a differentiator between great and poor salesmen.

Even in antiquity, long before marketing was a formal discipline, personal branding and selective language were a centerpiece of the sales process. Products came to be held in high regard due to their creator, locale, or any other kind of marketable attribute. Language was to marketing and bartering as a camera is to film: a vital tool in its creation and process.

As far back as ancient Egypt, brands arose from whispers and gossip. The wealthy defined themselves by the products they had access to, much like people do today. They were given feelings of superiority and exclusivity when they commanded the names of their favorite vase maker, food provider, or fish sauce manufacturer. But it wasn't just the names of the products; it was the language that came with them. It was the use of slogans like "the flower of," "Finger Lickin' Good," and "Just Do It." And more than this, it was the concepts and conventions laid beneath those slogans—most importantly, the emotions that they inspired.

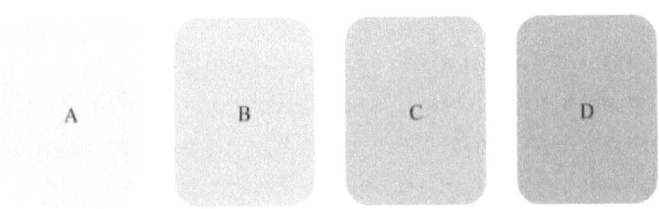

"The Gambling Task" involves four decks of cards being laid out, each with their own odds of success.

Imagine that you're sat at a table with four decks of cards in front of you. Each deck is labeled, from left to right, A, B, C, D. You're asked to pick a card from the top of one of the decks—the choice is up to you. You decide to start from the left: deck A. You pick up a card. On the top, it says that you've won $50. You place the card next to you, happy with your $50. You're then asked to pick up another card. You decide to take one from deck B. This time, though, it says that you lose $50.

You're again asked to pick up a card. You decide to go with deck D. You win $100. As you are asked again and again to pick up a card, you find that decks C and D tend to offer higher rewards, while A and B offer lower rewards. However, C and D also tend to take away more money, while A and B take less. The question you're left asking yourself is: which decks do you take from to gain the most money?

For most individuals, the answer to that question is a judgment call. It's a decision based on how much risk you feel is worth it. However, when neuroscientist Antonio Damasio performed this experiment on patients with impaired emotional ability, he found that they showed no significant leaning one way or another. [3] In other words, their inability to assign emotional relevance to any of the decks meant they were unable to make reasoned decisions as to which ones they should favor.

To make decisions, then, emotion is a vital part of the underlying machinery. It is required to judge the different options made available to the decision-maker and decide on the most beneficial one. For the experiment's participants, this decision was which deck to pick a card from. For consumers, this decision is whether to purchase or not to purchase; to buy from one brand or to buy from another.

When Roman consumers heard a slogan of Scaurus's fish sauce, it wasn't the slogan itself that encouraged them to make the decision to purchase. Rather, that language acted as a tool for changing the concepts and conventions of consumers, with the aim of evoking specific emotions. The fact that the name Umbricius was associated with the fish sauce drew connotations of opulence and quality, and that it was described as a flower implicated a pleasant smell and taste. Both of these evoked the emotions of optimism and interest and thereby secured consumer purchasing decisions.

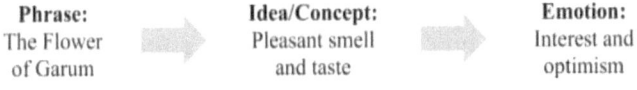

Phrase:	Idea/Concept:	Emotion:
The Flower of Garum	Pleasant smell and taste	Interest and optimism

The process of language to emotion.

Language is powerful because it is more than just a way for us to communicate with one another. It influences how we think and how we see the world and, as a result, influences the decisions we make. In other words, when used deftly, language can make people want to buy because it emotionally resonates.

Let's look at another example of how language can influence decision-making. Imagine that the world was facing one of the worst viral outbreaks it has ever seen. You are a virologist, studying the virus and looking for a cure. After months of trial and error, you find a serum that works on fifty percent of those infected. This will mean that fifty percent of the human race will survive. Do you administer it, or continue working to find something better?

Now let's reframe that question: The world is facing one of the worst viral outbreaks it has ever seen. After months of trial and error, the best you can do is a serum that works on fifty percent of those infected. Due to the scale of the outbreak, this means that half of the remaining population will die. Do you administer it?

When questions like these were asked by two University of Chicago psychologists in 2012, they found that the first outcome was almost always preferable when participants used their first language. [4] This is even though both outcomes are the same. In both cases, half of the population dies, except in the first example it is phrased as half of the population surviving. So why is the first outcome more favorable?

The reason is, ultimately, ethics: socially acceptable moral principles for governing our behavior. Participants believed that the positively framed outcome was ethically acceptable, while the negatively framed outcome was not. Yet when we consider that both outcomes were logically the same, it doesn't make sense that ethics would dictate that one of the outcomes is better than the other. But it does when we consider how language can influence an individual's choices. The language used to frame the first outcome was positive, and as a result it evoked more positive emotions. The language used to frame the second outcome was negative, and as a result it evoked more negative emotions. The foundation of these choices—ethics—is based on socially accepted norms the participants were brought up with. The first outcome isn't only more emotionally positive; it also resonates more strongly with those accepted norms.

The study shows the degree to which social and discourse conventions are wrapped up in our language—even when those choices don't make logical sense. It shows how norms, concepts, and conventions are central to our ability to make choices, and how slight changes can influence our answers.

I'm often reminded of a series of HSBC advertisements that played almost twenty years ago. In these ads, the slogan "the world's local bank" was reinforced with information about cultural differences around the world. From the perspective of an outsider, the ads were quirky and interesting. They often provided knowledge that individuals found interesting. For example, that Americans always conduct business meetings while standing up, or that it's important not to finish what's on your plate in China. What these individuals didn't know—me included—was that most of the "facts" presented in the adverts were, in fact, terrible and incorrect stereotypes. [5]

For those watching the ads, though, this didn't matter. HSBC was an authoritative source. It was, after all, the world's local bank. HSBC could have created an entire mythos around foreign cultures and the majority of their viewership would have done little more than bat an eyelid. However, as that viewership watched the advertisement, their understanding of the world changed. Whether correct or not, they began to believe that it was important to leave food on your dish in China and that Americans all conducted business while standing up.

For the ancient Pompeiians, the idea of fish sauce smelling was something they expected. Even with factories confined to the outskirts of cities, away from residential and business districts, word of mouth would spread knowledge about the smells they would create. And even if they had not heard of the smells through word of mouth, they would likely have associated the idea of fish sauce with the smells they would experience at the local fish market.

So when they heard Scaurus's slogan "the flower of," what they heard was that his fish sauce was uniquely pleasant. That it wasn't just any old fish sauce, but a fish sauce worthy of being imported all the way to France. What they heard was language that changed their underlying ideas and conventions around fish sauce, and so their emotional attachment to it.

So why is language so important for marketers? For the same reason that individuals favor outcomes when framed positively, trust HSBC despite its factual inaccuracies, or believe in the value of a fish sauce from the other side of the known world. It's important because it is able to influence how consumers perceive, make decisions, and attribute trust.

While Scaurus may have done something simple, the same ideas have continued to propagate throughout the marketing world. Today, businesses curate the language they use to create marketing campaigns that are convincing and purposeful. They then tie these campaigns together under the single banner of a brand. This book is about how any business can do this. It's about how they can use language to influence the way their consumers perceive, make decisions, and attribute trust. But most of all, it's about how you, as a marketer, can understand your brand so you can read and write using its own unique language.

2

The Coca Cola Shift

Everyone knows what Santa Claus looks like: a large, jolly man with a long, white beard running down the front of a red suit with white fur trim. For decades, the image has been everywhere at Christmas. It has been a vital part of Christmas advertisements, been central to the shopping center "grotto" experience, and defined a figure to whom children worldwide have written letters containing their Christmas wish lists.

But Santa hasn't always looked like this. His age, clothes, and temperament are all, primarily, a product of the 20th century. All of these facets of the character, which we often believe to be timeless, were only created within the last one hundred years.

For some, this may not come as a surprise. After all, an oft-cited urban legend states that Santa was not always dressed in the red garb we've come to love. Rather, as legend goes, he once wore a green suit, and the only reason we see him dressed in red is because of corporate appropriation by Coca-Cola. However, like most urban legends, this isn't true.

The artist behind Coca-Cola's famous representation of Santa—Haddon Sundblom—was not the first to paint him in red clothes. This honor belongs to artist Thomas Nast. But it's not hard to see why Nast's change was attributed to Sundblom and Coca-Cola. While Nast may have changed the color of his clothes, it was really Sundblom who changed Santa into what we've come to expect today. His work, while based on that of other artists, was a powerful driving force behind Coca-Cola's 20th-century success.[1]

Santa Claus as depicted in 1920 with the red suit but a much less jolly temperament. [3]

But like all good things, Sundblom and Coca-Cola's reimagining of Santa didn't occur overnight. [2] It was the product of over a decade's worth of trial and error, starting in the 1920s when the first images of "Coca-Cola Santa" appeared in publications like *The Saturday Evening Post*.

These advertisements, while showing Santa donning the red-colored outfit we know and love, missed a vital component we've come to expect: joy. Instead of smiling, the Santa of the 1920s was solemn. He stared at his list, possibly pondering which children to provide presents for and which to give coal. But what he was not doing was grinning. That was about to change.

Fred Mizen's Jolly Santa

In 1930, artist Fred Mizen created an image showing a department store Santa drinking a bottle of Coke. The image looked much like the Santa of the 1920s, but there was one core difference: this Santa was jolly. Leaning backwards and taking a swig from a glass of Coke, it was clear that this Santa wasn't a solemn one.

The image was a hit, and the strict-looking Santa of the 1920s would soon become a thing of the past.

Just a year later, in 1931, Sundblom brought out the first mainstream image of the Santa we've all come to know and love: a smiling, jolly Santa. His work was the product of over a decade of careful measuring. For each image of Santa throughout the 1920s, what resonated and what didn't was recorded and refined. Every change—no matter how large or small—gave insight into what consumers wanted and what they expected. You might say that Sundblom's picture in '31 was inevitable.

Sundblom's Santa of '31

But why did it take so long? Why was it that more than a decade had to pass for Coca-Cola to adopt a jolly Santa? That question is especially relevant when we consider that Sundblom wasn't the first artist to draw Santa in the way we recognize him. As I already said, Thomas Nast was responsible for that.

The answer is probably that a lot of advertisers at the time didn't understand that convention change requires convention. Back then, marketing theories revolved around ideas similar to the hypodermic needle model—the concept that audiences would digest and internalize whatever you showed them. [4] The idea was that if you gave an audience a picture of your product and said that it would make their lives better, they would believe it. There was no room for audience interpretation, engagement, or the concept of trust.

We now know that this isn't how it works. Instead, meaning is arrived at through a "conversation" between the text and the audience. By understanding this, Sundblom and Coca-Cola managed to shift social conventions and align the brand of Coca-Cola with the brand of Christmas. Today, the image of Santa holding a bottle of Coke and grinning with rosy cheeks is one of Christmas's most recognizable images. You would be hard-pressed to get through the holiday season without seeing it at least once. And when you talk about Santa with your friends and family, you always mention that he's a jolly character.

Coca-Cola isn't the only brand to have done something like this. McDonald's was also responsible for reinventing and shifting convention. Except instead of changing a holiday character, they changed customer expectations.

If you don't know the story already, McDonald's wasn't always a huge corporation. In the beginning, it was just a small burger shop run by two brothers: Richard and Maurice McDonald. Ray Kroc then joined the company in 1955 as a franchise agent.

While the store started as a small, friendly burger joint, Kroc would eventually buy the company from the McDonald brothers in 1961. [5] Today, McDonald's is one of the largest fast-food chains in the world, serving over 69 million customers every day. They achieved this by doing something no one else did: they served burgers quickly.

David Hogan, a fast-food industry scholar, is quoted as saying that McDonald's is the marketer of the concept that hamburgers are American food. Not just any hamburger, though: the production-line hamburger. Ray Kroc's concept of the production-line hamburger was very much rooted in the concept of a quick burger. Much like how Coca-Cola changed conventions associated with the image of Santa and Scaurus changed conventions associated with the smell of fish sauce, McDonald's changed conventions associated with ordering food.

Today, the concepts of speed and instant gratification are everywhere we look. A mix of too much content, too little time, and deep-seated expectations set by organizations like McDonald's have fundamentally changed the way we interact with and engage with brands and products. It has become such a core staple in our society that almost all industries now have some form of instant gratification rolled into their marketing. Think about the last tech product you invested in. If you took a long, hard look at the language being used by that product, you would be hard-pressed not to find something regarding speed.

McDonald's changed convention by changing expectations. Coca-Cola changed convention by changing imagery. So where does language fit into this?

In 1947, how do you think people proposed to one another? Do you think they got down on one knee, pulled out a ring with a diamond on it, and presented it to their loved ones? They didn't, because proposing with diamonds wouldn't be a mainstream thing until 1948, when the diamond cartel De Beers released its first advert with the tagline "A Diamond Is Forever." [6]

Prior to 1948, diamonds were less about romance and more about extravagance. In fact, much of the diamond industry was in trouble due to almost two decades of the public not wanting to buy them. The Great Depression had meant people didn't have money for luxuries. Even before this, interest in shiny stones wasn't what it is today. So when Frances Gerety was asked for a slogan in 1947, the idea that it could change the industry forever probably didn't cross her mind.

Yet it did. A sentence that was grammatically incorrect and that no one was very excited about came to be associated with romance, marriage, and engagement. Just like Coca-Cola, Scaurus, and McDonald's, De Beers changed convention. And just like Coca-Cola and McDonald's, this change in convention manifested itself in language. For Coca-Cola, that was the language of their audience: they changed the language that made up Christmas by changing the image of Santa. For McDonald's, it was the language of their industry: they changed the language that was used in their industry by changing consumer expectations. For De Beers, it was the language of both: they changed how their industry talked about and sold diamonds, and they changed what diamonds meant to consumers.

These convention changes occur all around us, constantly. They are the driving force behind many of the largest and most successful companies. Instead of adopting a competitive mentality, these innovators decide to change the game entirely. Why did soft drinks just have to mean sustenance? Why did burgers just have to be meat and bread on a plate? Why were diamonds just something for rich people? By asking these questions and challenging the status quo, industries changed, and with them, so too did society.

But again, these changes did not take place overnight. They were implemented slowly—and, in most cases, haphazardly. Today, Coca-Cola uses penguins and polar bears in their advertisements. How do you think this would have gone down in 1931?

The answer lies in how humans cognitively cope with uncertainty. According to neuroscientists David Rock and Al Ringleb, uncertainty registers in the brain much like an error does. This creates a feeling of discomfort, one which doesn't go away until the brain has adjusted and everything seems "right" again. But that discomfort eases over time—even when the odds are stacked against us. In fact, we can be facing the proposition of complete loss and still accept it with some degree of comfort—if the run-up has been long enough.

In a study of long-shot gambling behavior, researchers found that gamblers were more likely to bet on long odds the longer they experienced a losing streak. The reasoning, however, wasn't that gamblers were looking to recoup losses. Rather, it was that gamblers became accustomed to losing and so were more accepting of the higher potential to lose with long-shot odds. [7]

If Coca-Cola had used penguins or polar bears in their advertisements in 1931, they almost certainly would have been met with uncertainty, confusion, and rejection. What has made Coca-Cola's strategy work is that they embraced the long game and the concept of turn-taking.

In 2005, David Crystal talked about how individuals need to feel like they are taking part in an interaction. It is the individual's need to be heard that fuels the direction of conversation. That participation isn't just verbal. In many cases, it can be non-verbal interactions and displays. For the Coca-Cola campaign, it was reactionary. When Coca-Cola released an ad and the response was negative or flat, Coca-Cola then responded with a different one—one that was similar but slightly different. When the response was positive, they responded with a campaign that was similar.

In this way, turn-taking occurs in almost all of society's interactions. It's surprising that, even today, many marketers seem to dismiss the importance of turn-taking in engaging with their audience. Imagine you were talking to a friend. Would that interaction be one-sided? If it was, that friendship probably wouldn't last. Instead, what should happen is one person speaks, the other listens, then they switch.

The same should occur in marketing. The brand speaks, the customer listens. Then the customer speaks, and the brand listens and reacts. It's the stage of brand reaction that led to Coca-Cola making a move that cut through the noise in 1931. It's how McDonald's changed convention with its production-line burgers in the 1950s that now define American cuisine. And it's the reason why De Beers waited a year to use the slogan "A Diamond Is Forever." When it was created, the public just wasn't ready for it—whether De Beers were aware of that or not.

Each of these brands listened to their audience. Each of them negotiated a shared meaning—one that spoke to both the gratification requirements of the audience and the business requirements of the company. By gradually shifting convention in a specific direction, companies like Coca-Cola can now show polar bears and penguins, fast-food chains like McDonald's can continue to grow, and De Beers can continue to make lots and lots and lots of money.

As a linguistic marketer, it is your job to create a framework for these shifts: a strategy. Trial and error are an integral part of this, but with the right tools at your disposal, a comprehensive strategy can help you to achieve the results you want in a far shorter time period.

Part 2

How We Perceive Brand

*The scientific mind does not so much
provide the right answers as ask the
right questions.*

- Claude Lévi-Strauss

3

How Does Language Work?

In 1965, Noam Chomsky pioneered the concept of Universal Grammar, a theory which stated that there exists a genetically hard-coded mechanism behind the language of all human beings. For Chomsky, this meant that regardless of circumstance, geography, or any one of several other factors, every single person around the world should show core similarities in the way they process language. It was a radical theory, but at the time, a lot of academics agreed with it because, in the most extreme sense, Chomsky's theory said that the language of all humans is fundamentally the same. It was hard for many academics to see beyond their own comprehension of language.

Since 1965, numerous linguists have come forward to say that Chomsky's theory is incorrect. Languages have been found that are entirely dissimilar from one another. They have different syntaxes, different grammars, and different methods for communicating. In fact, if you look far and wide enough, it's entirely possible to find languages that are so dissimilar from English that it would take decades to master their fundamentals. So when, almost a decade ago, I wrote an essay entitled *Can Pictures Assert?*, it's not surprising that I quickly found myself writing an essay about language. [1]

The question, despite using the word "pictures," was really asking about the nature of language. After all, from a cognitive perspective, images speak to us just as much as words on a page or voices over the radio. They all provide us with some form of input that we then convert into meaning: all three are forms of language. However, it's the conversion part where things get tricky. It's not enough to simply say whether a picture can assert or not; we have to ask ourselves why a picture can assert, and—if it can—what it can assert.

When it boils down to it, the question is really asking, "what is language?" Is it something innate to its source, or does it require external knowledge? If it's innate to its source, then can images assert anything, or do they require something else to have meaning? Can the picture I took of my family last week assert anything? Can the picture I took of my friend's dog assert anything

What action is this man performing?

Take a look at the image. If I were to ask you what the man is doing, what would you say? Chances are, you would say that the man is riding his bike. And you would be correct, but that's not the answer a German speaker would give.

At least, that's what a team of linguistic researchers found when they explored how German-English bilinguals described the actions of individuals. [2] After showing participants short clips of people performing specific actions, such as walking towards a car or cycling to a market, the participants were then asked to describe what was happening. It was found that when speaking German, individuals were much more likely to describe the motion (walking) and the goal (to the car). English speakers tended to only describe the motion. In other words, the same image was read in two different ways by two different groups of people.

Considering this, what can the image really tell us? After all, did you—reading this in English—even consider where the man was cycling to?

When Umbricius Scaurus decided on his slogan, it didn't have an innate meaning, just like when De Beers decided to go with the line "A Diamond Is Forever." Instead, both marketing campaigns linked their products to a concept. Nice-smelling fish sauce was not the exclusive domain of Scaurus; he did not invent the concept of nice smells. And diamonds as an engagement gift were not the exclusive domain of De Beers. Similarly, Coca-Cola did not create the first image of a jolly Santa. In 1881, Thomas Nast drew Santa as a jolly character for the poem *A Visit From St. Nicholas*. That's 50 years before Coca-Cola's ad campaign was launched. They did not own Jolly Santa, but they did cause him to become a social convention.

All of these concepts already existed before the brands used them. Instead of saying that the brands created the concepts their campaigns were built on, it makes more sense to say the concepts came from social conventions (concepts) modified by the brands. Coca-Cola saw that there was an opportunity to use the image of a jolly Santa to improve its business. De Beers saw that there was an opportunity to use engagement and marriage conventions to improve sales. And Scaurus saw that there was an opportunity to label his fish sauce as smelling pleasant.

Similar to the study of the English-German speakers, the meaning of the campaigns—including the slogans— was not innate. In the study, the speakers interpreted the meaning of the images differently based on the cultural conventions they had access to. For the brands, consumers similarly interpreted the images based on the social conventions and concepts they already had access to.

Assuming this is correct, and language is the product of interpretation, where does meaning actually come from? To understand this, we have to look at semiotics.

Semiotics is the study of signs, symbols, and their relationship to one another. [3] Signs and symbols, in this context, make up more than just stop, go, or any other range of road signs you're accustomed to on your morning commute. Rather, signs and symbols are anything that has meaning attached to it as a result of external influences.

Take, for instance, the English alphabet. Each of the letters of the alphabet is a sign of a particular phoneme—its sound. It does not mean that sound innately; otherwise, everyone around the world would pronounce words in the same way. Rather, the sound associated with the image (letter) comes from what we are taught from a young age. The meaning of a letter is dependent on social and discourse conventions— influenced by geographical location, social group, context, and more.

What this means is that letters and words are pronounced differently by an American businessman in a meeting than by a British blue-collar worker at the pub. We know this is the case. We even have a word for it: dialect. [4]

Assuming this as true, we can then see that the question "can a picture assert?" is the same as "can language assert?" Both questions cause us to ask what the relationship between the sign and its meaning is.

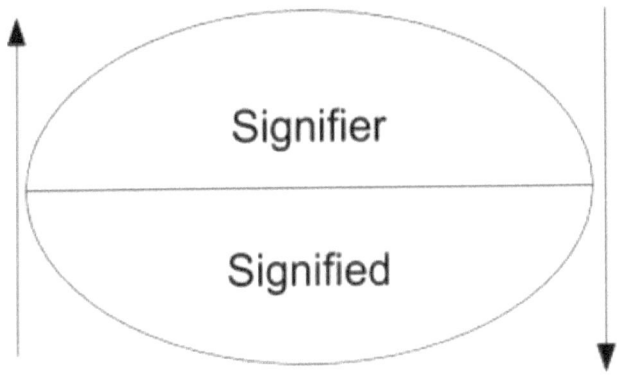

Ferdinand de Saussure's depiction of the Signifier and Signified. [5]

Ferdinand de Saussure talked about signs in detail. In fact, he created the idea of the signifier and the signified, which he said combine to create what we call a sign.

If we take the example of a stop sign, the sign itself is the signifier, while the meaning "stop" is the signified. The sign is the two concepts together. With the alphabet, the signifier is the letter, while the sound is the signified; combined, they form the sign. The letter "a" (signifier) and the sound "ahhh" (signified) combine and become a sign.

In semiotics, this relationship exists almost everywhere and in everything we see. Take an image from a quit-smoking campaign. Without accompanying text, does that image have meaning?

"Of course!" is what most people would say. The image of a blackened set of lungs must surely assert that smoking is bad for you, right? Millions of dollars have been put into researching images since smoking prevention ad campaigns started. There must be a reason why those images were chosen and not, say, cute pictures of cats.

In order to know why specific images are used in quit-smoking campaigns, we must move beyond Saussure's model. While it exposes the meaning itself and what signifies that meaning, it does not consider where meaning comes from. Does the meaning come from the signifier itself? Is the letter "a" innately the sound "ahhh"? Does the inclusion of "think" in the sentence "I think I like eating ice cream" act innately as a hedging device? Does a picture of a set of black lungs assert that smoking is bad for you? Or do these things imply; do these things indicate to specific individuals?

When confronted with the stop-smoking campaign, an individual must first know what smoking is. Cigarettes themselves were not a widespread phenomenon until the 20th century. If they had not become as widespread as they are today, would we even know what a cigarette was by looking at it? They must then know what a set of lungs looks like. Modern human anatomy only became a thing in the 16th century, when Andreas Vesalius took a detailed look at the different systems that make up the human body. Before this, how often do you think an average person would have seen a pair of lungs? Do you think the average 10th-century individual would know what a set of lungs looks like?

As the famous linguist Umberto Eco once wrote in his work *The Name of the Rose*: *stat rosa pristina nomine, nomina nuda tenemus* ("the rose of old remains only in name; we possess bare names"). [6]

The argument here is that because being able to "read" images requires external knowledge, the reading of a text must ultimately be individual. For many modern linguists, this point of view holds true. Language is no more fixed or innate than acquired characteristics. With this view in mind, linguist Roman Jakobson came up with his own model of communication: one that considered more than just the signifier and the signified.

Jakobson's model allowed for individuals to create their own units of meaning from personal influences. It included influences from more than the message itself. The context around the message was important, as was the channel it was delivered through and any codes shared between the addresser and the addressee. In Jakobson's model, meaning is the product of context, metalingual elements, the discourse conventions used, and a compromise between the addresser and the addressee.

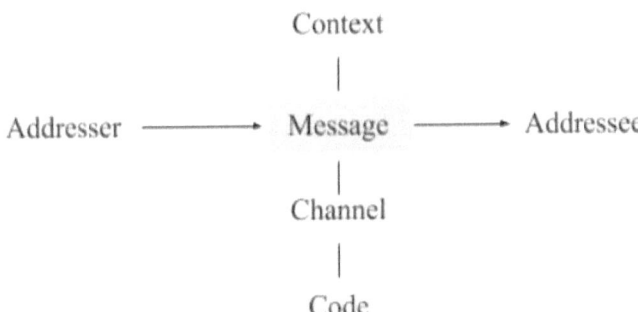

Jakobson's model of communication.

This means much more than just that meaning is the product of external knowledge. Jakobson's model means there is a complex scale of ideas that allow individuals to interpret the same image in different ways and to different extents. For a person diagnosed with cancer due to smoking, the quit-smoking image would likely have a more intense meaning than for someone who has never smoked a day in their life.

For McDonald's, the concept of the fast burger was a product of a society that was constantly rushing to get things done, where time was as much of a commodity as money. For Coca-Cola, a jolly Santa was likely motivated by a desire for Christmas to be a happy, jolly time of year. For De Beers, diamonds becoming a mainstream engagement gift was likely the product of a society that looked for new ways to prove commitment between lovers. In order to create meaning, all of these campaigns relied on external knowledge and existing conventions. They simply tweaked them a little.

Jakobson's model was far from the final adaptation to Saussure's original, but what it did was bring added depth to the notion that meaning was pulled from more than just the sign itself. It started to build a picture of how we understand and engage with language as individuals, and the importance of social and discourse conventions in constructing meaning.

So can images assert? Yes and no. Yes, in that every individual who looks at an image sees meaning, but no in that the meaning they see comes from knowledge outside of the image. There is more at play than just the signifier and the signified. The letter "a" does not inherently mean the sound "ahh"; "Santa Claus" does not inherently mean jolly.

For marketers, an awareness of this—and how to manipulate it—is key to creating successful campaigns: ones that are both psychologically resonant and inspire action. As we'll talk about in more detail in the next chapter, convention is a tool through which marketers are able to create content that an audience will follow. It's also something that can be used to build incredibly powerful relationships and connections between brands and the real world.

4

The Origin of Meaning

Imagine you were one of the first people to see the Santa Claus advertisement released by Coca-Cola in 1931. Also imagine that it was the first time you had ever heard of Coca-Cola. What would you think? Would the image of a jolly-looking Santa encourage you to switch your carbonated beverage of choice to Coca-Cola, or would you dismiss it?

Now imagine that the following year you saw the image again, this time with a few minor changes. Your friend mentions, as a joke, that Coca-Cola is the drink of Santa Claus. Another friend dresses up as Santa for the big day, and they opt for the Coca-Cola version of Santa—it was the only outfit at the store. Over the next few years, times get tougher and a fairly bad recession kicks in. Coca-Cola releases an image of Santa with the line "Me too!" next to it. Everyone is still happy, and Coca-

Cola is still being brought to families. The following year, an advertisement shows up that depicts children leaving Coca-Cola out for Santa instead of the traditional milk. Your kid thinks it's fun, and so that year you get a glass of Coke when you're laying out the presents for the next morning. Over the years, your idea of Coca-Cola changes. You go from not knowing what it is to thinking of it as a brand that understands and inspires happiness: happiness that you want. You've now become a Coca-Cola drinker, and we haven't even considered advertisements outside of the holidays.

The journey above takes you from a potential customer who knows nothing about a brand to a loyal customer who has bought into its promise. Coca-Cola managed to get the product into your social circle by releasing ad campaigns that targeted real situations your social group was encountering. They then managed to influence your family and change the tradition of leaving milk out on Christmas Eve. But as these things happened, what motivated you to make the move from a potential customer to a loyal customer? Why were the ad campaigns so powerful, and why was your friend dressing up as Coca-Cola Santa and your kid asking to leave out Coca-Cola instead of milk important?

Social conventions are the ideas that we pick up throughout our lives; the knowledge we gain from experiences and reflection. Within linguistic research, social conventions can include "knowledge, attitudes and ideologies, and [other] representations of the social mind." [1] In other words, anything that is an interpretation of reality as a result of an individual's existing knowledge.

Over time, these ideas combine to create generalizations about the world around us and how we should act. Brands sometimes try to take control of these ideas and generalizations to create connections that we may otherwise dismiss. In fact, great brands create texts that act as a catalyst for change to social convention and its connection to everyday life.

In 2016, laundry detergent company Ariel released an advertising campaign in India that did just that. The campaign featured a mother returning home from work and then trying to tend to several daily chores. She makes food, she cleans the house, she washes her family's clothes. She does all this while her husband sits on the couch watching TV. Her father, also present, watches her perform these tasks and narrates an apology for allowing her to play house as a child, and believing that the woman should do all the work. The ad ends with the line "why is laundry only a mother's job".

The advertisement was a powerful testament to a brand's ability to change social conventions. Millions of men spoke up on social media, promising to #SharetheLoad, and sales for Ariel's line of washing detergent rose 60 percent.

It did this because there was already a social convention in place for more equality in the home. India already had a belief that men should do more of the housework. The ad campaign was a complete success because it understood that existing social convention. It then took control of it and changed it in a way that the brand's audience wanted.

Coca-Cola transformed social convention regarding Santa's appearance. McDonald's changed social convention regarding the wait time for a burger. De Beers changed social convention regarding suitable occasions for diamonds. All three managed to change social convention in a way that created a connection with their brand: that placed their brand within a particular social canon. They all did this by telling a story and by appealing to emotion and desire.

The role of emotion and desire in marketing is no secret. If you create content that resonates with an audience, then you must be creating content that acts as a catalyst of desire. When Umbricius Scaurus created his slogan "the flower of", it appealed to a desire: his customers wanted fish sauce that didn't smell bad. When Ariel created the #SharetheLoad campaign, they appealed to a desire for more equality in the home. Coca-Cola did this with Santa, McDonald's did this with its speedy burger, and De Beers did this with diamonds. Each brand drew a connection from its brand to social conventions by using emotion.

There is one brand that has been more successful at this than almost any other: Nike.

Nike was founded in 1964 by track athlete Phil Knight. Then known as Blue Ribbon Sports (BRS), the brand had humble origins. Knight, wanting to increase brand awareness but not sure how, made most of his sales at track meets out of the back of his car. His tactic worked, and by the end of his second year, he had made over $20,000. The business continued to grow and expand as Knight grew operations outside of his home state of Oregon. Over the years, Nike became a well-known sports apparel brand whose shoes were thought of as high-quality running shoes with a unique waffle design. That all changed in 1988 when Nike revolutionized its own branding with an advert that focused on the brand instead of the product. This wasn't the first brand ad Nike had launched, but it was the most powerful.

The first Nike "brand" ad—featuring no actual Nike products—was released in 1977 and was created by an advertising agency called John Brown and Partners. The first pre–"Just Do It" slogan was born: "There Is No Finish Line." Despite being a catchy line that aligned with the conventions that would ultimately come to define Nike, it was not powerful enough to fully resonate.

Instead, what the slogan did do was open a conversation with Nike's audience; a conversation the public answered by rising to action and purchasing more and more shoes. By December of 1980, just three short years after the release of Nike's brand ad, they had achieved a 50 percent market share in the US athletic shoe market. They had "just done it."

For almost a decade, Nike as a brand grew to dominate the US market. Instead of sitting securely on its branding victories, it continued to communicate with its customers. Its marketing team pushed ad campaigns that saw the brand addressing social issues. They pushed for female and class inclusion, they supported the "little guy", and they addressed societal fears. Each of these campaigns contributed to the overall social conventions associated with Nike—they built generalizations that enabled the potential for connections. Without the brand identity these constructed, Nike's most powerful slogan would probably have fallen flat. Priming its audience was vital.

The "Just Do It" slogan appeared in 1988. A clear call to action by the brand, the line brought together countless disparate voices and individuals, and told them that they—as individuals—were capable of doing anything. It targeted all Americans—regardless of age, gender, or physical fitness level. It was a personal message to the customer. It talked to the multitude of challenges and obstacles they faced every day. And it said that those obstacles were nothing when they wore Nike.

This connection was not innate to the Nike product. In fact, it's arguable that Nike shoes are much the same as any other sports shoes, bearing no real distinction other than the brand. So how did Nike take a product much like any of its competitors' and transform it into a brand that spoke to the individual with an intensely complex message?

They used social convention.

The advertisement featured Walt Stack, an 80-year-old American who ran 17 miles every morning. At the time, he was already famous and regarded as a San Francisco "institution". In fact, more than 10 years earlier, in 1975, *Sports Illustrated* had published a piece on Walt Stack entitled "The Old Man and the Bay". [2]

The advert was short—just 30 seconds—but in those 30 seconds Nike managed to communicate that it was for everyone, doing anything, and that they believe you can

Just Do It too. An 80-year-old man "just does it"—so can you. Through shifting the social conventions associated with sports apparel, they changed the game from one of just shoes to shoes that gave you the power to do anything. Today, Nike is synonymous with the idea of success—especially within the context of sports.

This is the power of social convention and how language links to promoting and evolving a product. By knowing existing social convention and making subtle but powerful changes in a kind of dialogue with your audience, you're able to create a brand that does more than just sell a product. You're able to make a brand that changes society.

Discourse Convention

Take a look at a Nike advertisement from this year and compare it to a Nike advertisement from the 1960s. Everything is different. From font to images, tone to style. Even the language. The two advertisements do not look the same.

You may be thinking that this is just the gradual evolution of Nike's marketing efforts. To a certain degree, you would be right. However, take a look at other ads from the 1960s. Immediately, you should notice that some features seem very similar. Each of them uses similar formats, similar-style images, and even similar linguistic features. What you're noticing is called discourse convention.

Discourse convention is the way in which discourse is created. It involves everything from the language used to the images and design that support that language. Discourse conventions are anything that doesn't seem "out of place" when placed alongside contemporaneous texts. Take a look at action movie posters. You'll notice a lot of them have similar elements and color schemes. This is because it is dictated by discourse convention.

Discourse convention, just like social convention, can change. Just the fact that advertisements of the 1960s and today are so different shows this. What's expected and easily digested by the public one day is completely different the next. What needs to be easy to understand one year may be better served as a complex campaign during a different year. In other words, the marketing stories we are told change not in terms of structure, but in terms of the elements that they are made up of.

Each advertisement you see shows specific discourse conventions. Take the Nike ad. It was 30 seconds long, it contained only a handful of lines of dialogue, and it told a very simple story. The viral Ariel advertising campaign, however, contained more dialogue and required the use of multi-channel integration between social channels (with hashtags) and television advertisements. It's not just smaller elements that change; it's formats too. For Coca-Cola, the print-based ad was its bread and butter. For Nike, it was video. These different formats were arguably the discourse conventions of their times, as was the fact that Nike's video was brand-focused and not product-focused. A brand-focused video would not have been understood in the 1960s.

Discourse conventions are also similar to social conventions in that they represent in-group and out-group dynamics. They are the product of a "broadly agreed set of common public goals, as well as [shared] values and beliefs that define [a] community." In other words, discourse convention is a great way for businesses to carve out and connect with unique communities of advocates.

Mint.com is a good example of this. An online money management tool that was first released in 2006, when Mint.com entered into the banking and financial industry, it was up against some big players. In most cases, businesses here fail to succeed, largely because the money behind the bigger businesses often drowns out any marketing and engagement efforts from smaller businesses. Mint.com, however, grew its user base to 1 million users in just under a year. After four years, it had over 10 million users, and it did it all with minimal investment. It did this by looking at what was unique to the discourse conventions of its industry.

If you look at different brands in different industries, you start to notice that the discourse conventions aren't the same. Dominant formats and channels change, as do tone and style. These changes are based on the audiences brands target. No one exists in every space. The banking industry is no different. In order for brands to get the most out of their marketing efforts, they try to redirect marketing spend towards areas their customers frequent. Historically, banks had spent money delivering ads through online channels and television. But just because brands see success through certain channels and with certain messaging doesn't mean there are no other unexplored opportunities out there.

Soon after Mint.com was successful, its founder Aaron Patzer said that "Ideas are really nothing; it's all in the execution of that idea." Today, when we think about entrepreneurs, we tend to think that their ideas must be good; that they must be ideas that stick with us and are needed. However, when Patzer asked his friends about Mint.com, only one said they would actually use it. Arguably, you could say that Patzer's idea was terrible and that it didn't have any audience. But then, Mint.com now has over 20 million users.

Patzer made his idea a success by doing one vital thing. He switched his marketing strategy from being one that relied on paid online and television advertisements, which were incredibly expensive, and instead focused on organic, digital experiences. This flaunted the discourse conventions of the banking industry and realigned what they meant for financial brands.

One of the ways he did this was with frequent and updated blog content. Blogs are a great resource for businesses looking to reframe and rebrand themselves. Not only do great blogs remove the hard-sell component from the mix, they also talk to customers on a more personal level. Instead of targeting middle-class families, Mint.com targeted up-and-coming young people. Those who would, over the course of the next few years, start to earn significantly and were planning ahead. This not only meant changes to the format and channel the brand communicated with customers through, it also meant changes to the tone, style, and language the brand used.

What Mint.com did that was so incredible was that it found an audience on channels that had largely been unexplored by other brands in its industry. It created interesting and resonant content that connected with its audience, and it found a way to manipulate the discourse conventions of the banking and finance industry to grow a user base that would then go on to promote the brand on the social level. In other words, it used content strategy to bring its brand to life for its users.

5

Creating a Story

When Nike created its "Just Do It" slogan, it didn't create it in a vacuum. Numerous ads were created before the 1988 Walt Stack video. There was the 1977 "There Is No Finish Line" brand advertisement targeting the middle class. There was the "Yankee way" ad targeting the working class. There was the 1980 Joan Benoit "Be as tough as she is" ad targeting females. And countless more advertisements targeted unique groups through carefully positioning copy and images to relate to them. Individually, they provided a message. Together, they provided a story.

It was because of this strategy that when the Walt Stack ad appeared on TV screens in 1988, the Nike audience was more primed than ever to accept its message and commit to the action of purchasing. Just like with the slow burn of the Coca-Cola Santa Claus story, Nike built up message on top of message; ones that were supported by the gradual acceptance of the Nike brand by different groups. Instead of a friend dressing up as Santa, he wore Nike shoes. Instead of your kid asking to put Coke out for Santa during Christmas, he asks for the latest pair of Nike shoes. The Walt Stack ad was the climax of the Nike story, and while the brand has continued to develop its messaging ever since, it has never strayed far from the message of "you can do anything."

The reason this works is because language does not exist in a vacuum. It is almost always a part of something bigger than itself. The ad from De Beers that featured the slogan "A Diamond Is Forever" is not the only thing that motivated men to buy diamonds as engagement presents for their significant others. The male executive team behind the De Beers ad campaigns originally thought that Frances Gerety's slogan was terrible. It was grammatically incorrect, it was on the nose, and they didn't see how it could possibly resonate with women. But Gerety was in a unique position that allowed her to see what the male advertising executives could not; she understood the social conventions that would help her slogan gain traction, and as a result, she was able to craft language that could.[1] In other words, Gerety was able to understand the story of diamonds and the diamond industry, and use language to give the conventions of the diamond industry purpose.

In 1946, a year before Gerety was asked to create her famous slogan, De Beers published an advertisement much like the countless ones that had come before.

Instead of telling a marketing story, they told a fictional one. That story can be seen below.

> *A wave wings in to kiss a tranquil shore. Among its fellows, it alone shines with a special, spray-jeweled splendor—because it brings first message of her love. So some day will her diamond gleam unique among proud-blazing gems, alight with her own love's significance. That is why the engagement ring-stone that's to mark her married lifetime should be selected for its singular role. It need not be of many carats, for color, clarity, and cutting are as important as actual weight. You will need the judgement of a trusted jeweler.*

Today, we couldn't imagine a marketing campaign with such long prose. It goes against everything marketers are taught and contradicts the idea of a fast-paced world where individuals have short attention spans. Long prose is the number one no-no of the copywriting world. But focusing on its length ignores larger, more fundamental issues with the text.

Robert McKee and Thomas Gerace write about the difference between the traditional story and the marketing story in their book *Storynomics*. They state that "a fiction story wraps a tight circle of involvement around its audience; the purpose-told story breaks that circle." [2] In other words, a fiction story finishes by satisfying its audience, while a marketing story finishes by encouraging a customer to purchase. For McKee and Gerace, the purpose of their story is to inspire action: to create movement.

Gerety's slogan didn't complete the story. Her line wasn't "he gave her a diamond and they stayed together forever." Instead, she gave the reader a call to action; one that lined up with existing conventions surrounding diamonds and their role in society. Not only that, but it lined up with the existing story that had been created by the industry. Whether knowingly or not, Gerety used language to create a catalyst that inspired action.

And it's for this reason that looking at advertising stories with a keen eye is so important. Look at the De Beers advert above and ask yourself how it lines up with your idea of a story.

At its core, a story has several parts. There is a setting, there are characters, there is a plot, there is a conflict, and there is a resolution. For McKee and Gerace, however, a marketing story should not have a resolution, not until a character has performed an action outside of the text.

To do this, the marketing story makes the reader its central character; its protagonist. It is then only the reader who is capable of achieving the resolution—the consumer. The story in the 1946 De Beers advert did not do this. The single line "A Diamond Is Forever" does. It does because it not only communicates meaning but does so in a way that a consumer can relate to and that resonates with their experience. As a result, it can inspire action.

Social Actors

During the creation of all stories, five things remain constant: setting, plot, conflict, resolution, and characters. As we just touched on, arguably the most important to the marketing story are the characters. More specifically, the character that is capable of bringing a resolution to the marketing story: the protagonist.

All stories revolve around characters. But no matter how many characters you have, at the center there will always be at least one protagonist. The protagonist is the character who ultimately brings about a story's resolution. The protagonist is the single most important character to the story, for without them the story would not exist. This is especially true of marketing stories.

In the 1946 De Beers advert, the protagonist was the diamond. The "engagement ring-stone" made the story's primary action. It marked the married woman. It wasn't the married woman (the desired target audience of the piece) who was committing the action. It was the diamond that did everything. It was the diamond that showed agency.

In the world of linguistics, agency is given to characters who commit actions. Characters that show agency are called social actors. This can be an individual, a group, or a collective. [3] When modern copywriters start out, they are often bombarded with advice: understand your niche, talk to your audience in their language, and always use the word "you." The reason they are told to use the word "you" is because it signifies that the reader is the main character. In other words, it tells the consumer that they are the one capable of fulfilling the marketing story and bringing about its resolution. However, the word "you" is not needed to do this. In fact, there are many different ways to provide agency to the reader that make a marketing text inspire action. The important thing to remember is that anyone can do something to a customer, but what can the customer do with the product?

When Gerety's slogan "A Diamond Is Forever" was released in 1948, one of the reasons for its popularity was its radical departure from the long-form prose of De Beers' earlier campaigns. Yet at the same time, it's important to remember that omission is not exclusion and addition is not inclusion. What this means is that just because a person or character is not explicitly mentioned in a text does not mean that they are not present. Gerety's slogan included the consumer as an agent of agency.

When Gerety came up with her line, she needed something that was going to stick; something that gave her audience the agency it needed to make the purchasing decisions De Beers wanted. Her slogan, built on her knowledge of the industry and its history, did exactly this. In one line, she summarized what the industry had been saying for some time, and she created a catalyst event that finally gave women agency in their own marriages. "A Diamond Is Forever" became "your marriage is forever," which became "you can make sure your marriage lasts forever by making your partner buy a diamond."

We've seen this effect in other marketing texts as well. Nike did this extremely well with its slogan "Just Do It," often parodied as "just buy it." This simple line does exactly what Gerety's did in 1948: it included the customer as the protagonist by omission. Sure, the real meaning of the line could have been "Jack can Just Do It" or "Lily will Just Do It." But because they omitted any clear protagonist, they included everyone. In the mind of the customer, the person who "will Just Do It" is them.

This isn't just limited to slogans either. McDonald's primary branding, as a fast burger, placed the customer as the protagonist: they were the ones enjoying the fast burger. When this no longer served its purpose, McDonald's became the American burger. Again, the American consumer was placed as protagonist and given agency over both the creation and consumption of McDonald's product. In fact, it's hard to find a product these days which doesn't revolve around its customer. And nowhere is that more visible than in a brand's tone and style.

Tone and Style

Tone and style have long underpinned marketing campaigns. They stretch beyond just content and have an influence on almost every area of a business's brand. If you were to look at an advert from McDonald's, or an employee's uniform, or a billboard advertisement, or any other product of the McDonald's marketing machine, you would likely instantly recognize the brand. The same is true of most big, modern brands.

Apple is a branding powerhouse, often talked about by branding experts. Today, it ranks as one of the largest technology companies in the world. It has consistently shown growth in the face of adversity, with global expansion and continued innovation of its products.

Simon Sinek, an organizational consultant, talked about Apple and its branding in his 2009 TED Talk: *How Great Leaders Inspire Action*. Here, he discussed the importance of a brand's why statement. Apple's, as he put it, was "With everything we do, we aim to challenge the status quo. We aim to think differently." Apple's brand is its why statement, and it is captured in both its tone and its style.

The Content Marketing Institute describes tone as "the content within your content. It carries all of the implicit messages about who you are, who your company is, and what your brand is all about." In other words, tone is the underlying message for all of your content. Perhaps this is the belief in something better; perhaps it is that you are the most knowledgeable, most adventurous, most innovative. There are a huge range of different ideas that tone can convey. Narrowing it down is the difficult part.

For Apple, the tone it settled on was innovation, and we can see it in everything it does. From the content on its website and the language choices it makes, to the unique layout of its stores and workplace culture. Apple strives to be innovative, not just in its marketing, but in its very nature as an organization.

Style, as the choice of language, directly impacts tone. It is more explicit, in that it's possible to deduce style quickly and easily by looking at a text. Take, for example, the Nike slogan "Just Do It." Here, the style is quick and to the point. It's a short sentence. In fact, all of the sentences in the 1985 ad are short. It says what it needs to say in just three words.

The tone of these three words, however, is much more complex. If we look at it from the perspective of attitude, those three words come with a force: a command. The attitude of Nike is empowerment. Its earlier attempts at slogans, such as the "There Is No Finish Line" ad in 1975, also used empowerment as a theme, albeit with less force. Linguistically, power here comes from directness. The use of short, to-the-point phrases, ones that are just three words long, is much better than using single negatives like "is no." The style of short sentences complements the tone of empowerment.

For Scaurus, whose fish sauce was known as "the flower of garum," his tone was one of opulence and affluence. His fish sauce would make you better, more prosperous. His style, however, was simple, especially if we account for the original Latin slogan. Instead of using the full Latin, he used abbreviations. "Gari Flos Scom" became "G F Sco." It is likely Scaurus did this on purpose to appeal to a particular audience: his consumers.

As we move into the final section of this book, know that choosing the right style is just as important as choosing the right tone. The language your brand chooses indicates to consumers the type of brand you are and what you believe in. It is here where the foundations of identification are created: *the language you use allows or disallows consumers to identify with your brand.*

6

The Feature Fallacy

Marketing effectively isn't easy. It often means digging into the fundamental aspects of a product and distilling that information into easily manageable chunks. While at first glance this may seem an easy task, many brands often get it wrong. They miss a piece of the puzzle. Sometimes it's as simple as effective communication channels. Other times, it's a failure to create stories that consumers can relate to. More often, it's not being able to replicate experiences that resonate. As a result, many brands run marketing campaigns that fail to truly inspire. Instead of inspiring action and driving conversions, they appeal only to those already likely to purchase.

Beyond simply creating stories, brands now have to create stories that speak to specific consumers. I've already touched on the role of the protagonist and the purpose of the marketing story. I've outlined how great, relatable marketing stories don't resolve themselves, but leave resolution open for the consumer to take action. In this way, an individual is not satisfied until they have made a purchase. Yet this isn't the only piece. Beyond stories lies another level; a level that takes something that can be seen as boring and uninspiring and supercharges it with emotion and meaning. This is the role of resonance.[1]

Resonance and relatability are similar concepts, but they are also slightly different. Relatability speaks to drawing associations. For example, in a campaign that focuses on football apparel, using imagery of football games is relatable to that audience. [2] Resonance, on the other hand, is about being able to have an impact. If that same football ad campaign showed a specific team, it may be resonant to supporters of that team, but not the supporters of another. In simple terms, relatability is about drawing connections, and resonance is about creating emotion. And when resonance and relatability mix, when a marketing story draws associations that have an impact, it begins to inspire. And when it then says something that matters, when it communicates an important message, that inspiration begins to drive action.

In 2016, Apple managed to change the phone market by driving home a relatable product with resonant messaging. They did this by ignoring what had already been positioned by competitors and recognizing the inability of those messages to inspire. Instead of talking about product specifications, features, and capabilities, they focused on the less tangible, but very resonant, benefits of the product. What I'm talking about is the rise of multiple cameras in smartphones.

Today, a flagship smartphone with only one camera is seen as an oddity. The dual camera, a feature that existed in only four percent of purchased smartphones in 2016, has grown to account for forty-two percent of the market in just two years. As of 2018, it's estimated that forty-six percent of smartphones sold globally include more than one camera. That's incredibly fast for such widespread adoption. [3]

But it wasn't that Apple was the first on the scene. Other brands had tried to sell dual camera smartphones in the past. HTC came out with the EVO 3D in 2011. LG also offered a multi-camera option in 2011: the Optimus 3D.[4] Both smartphones used multiple cameras to add depth to images, making them appear 3D. While the phones sold well, it wasn't because of the camera setup. And despite the brands continuing to work on the tech, it never took off.

Huawei then released the P9 in April 2016.[3] The second camera on the P9 was a wide-angle lens, designed to provide consumers with more flexibility in the types of shots they could take. Co-branded with the well-known and aspirational camera brand Leica, the P9 was popular and sold a lot of units in China. However, it just didn't resonate enough with average consumers to truly move the needle with regard to having more than one camera on a smartphone. It did not revolutionize the market.

Five months later, Apple released the iPhone 7, and dual cameras became the smartphone fixture that they are today.

But why did Apple manage to popularize multiple cameras where other smartphone providers didn't? It wasn't because of brand popularity. Huawei is equally as popular a brand in China, and HTC was one of the first brands to make a name for itself selling Android smartphones. It also wasn't that dual cameras were the next obvious step in smartphone evolution. The megapixel war was still raging, with manufacturers still trying to one-up each other in terms of image quality. [6]

Could it then have been the ecosystem of loyalty that Apple had built up, the almost mythological status of the brand? While this likely did have a role to play, it doesn't account for why so many Android manufacturers adopted similar technology when it would have been cheaper and easier to continue focusing on the megapixel war.

The main reason had to be that Apple had managed to make the concept of dual cameras resonate with the vast majority of consumers. Apple's marketing meant that consumers could understand the dual camera setup beyond just specification. The reason why Apple was successful where other brands fell flat is because of the language they used. Specifically, because their language focused on the benefit and not the feature.

If there is one thing you, as a marketer, take away from this book, it should be this. The way we perceive a brand is not in terms of its products. We don't choose and relate to Apple machines because of their processors, or Nike because of the materials it uses to make its shoes. Similarly, Scaurus' garum did not become popular because of the specific ingredients that were used in its creation. What made these brands the mainstream powerhouses they had and have become was that they spoke to the benefits they could provide a consumer; benefits that were relatable and that resonated and could inspire.

Before moving on to the third, and most important, section of this book, this chapter takes a moment to discuss the four key pillars of good content: communication, relatability, resonance, and inspiration. These four pillars make up the brand pyramid and seek to offer a clear checklist for how to create marketing campaigns that do more than just sell to those already ready to buy. They distinguish good content from bad content, and they form the basis for why brands like Apple succeed where others like Huawei fail.

Why Speed Doesn't Always Matter

"Everyone likes speed, right?"

That's what I kept hearing in the winter of 2016, when I worked at a small web hosting company. For years, they had been using speed as a pillar in all their marketing content: the speed of their servers, the speed of their connection, and the speed of getting started on their systems. The concept of speed underscored almost every marketing campaign that saw the light of day. But it wasn't working.

As business continued to spiral downwards, the team doubled down on efforts to make everything faster: "faster than the competition," "quicker than doing it yourself," "now even more optimized." Speed became such a totem for the brand that they started to build out product names around the concept of speed. They then marketed those products as being faster and quicker than any of the faster and quicker products they had created before. And the entire time they said their products were faster and quicker, the average consumer had no idea what to base that comparison on. It wasn't just that their language didn't resonate; it also wasn't relatable. After all, when you say that your servers are faster than those of your competition, what does that really mean to me, a consumer?

The problem was a disconnect between those who worked with the product day in and day out and those who purchased the product. When asked why their platform was better, those who developed the system used complex terminology to describe why. The marketing team then translated that into what they thought was relatable language. Most often, this ultimately fed into the concept of speed. And without really thinking about how they could drive truly powerful messaging, the team thought, "Everyone likes speed, right?"

For consumers, however, it didn't resonate. Speed was still a technical attribute, innately linked to the complex processes originally described by the developers. It wasn't even relatable. For each campaign that was successful, there were many more that fell flat and saw little to no spike in engagement. One particular campaign saw the company lose a substantial amount of investment after a message constructed around speed began to bizarrely resonate with individuals in admin roles who had zero influence on the technology decisions in their organization.

So in 2016, the brand took a new approach. Instead of communicating product-focused attributes, they began to develop and roll out consumer-resonant benefits. That is, they asked: What about this product specifically benefits consumers?

Speed quickly fell to the wayside. Market research showed that consumers wanted convenience, not speed. They wanted ease of use, not quicker setup times. And when it came to processing speed and power, the majority just wanted it to work. Hollow statements about speed and being "quicker" meant nothing to them, and detailed specifications citing the number of users a server could handle or processing speed performed even worse. By asking this question, the brand highlighted a critical flaw in its marketing. For years, it had promoted the features of its product and not the benefits it afforded consumers. There was a disconnect.

When HTC released the EVO 3D in 2011, it did the same. As its advertising campaigns rolled out, the camera feature was associated with one slogan.

Capture life in 3D.

Yes, it's a cool feature, and I'm sure many tech-savvy consumers looked forward to getting their hands on the new device. But how did its slogan communicate the benefits of the technology? Why does capturing things in 3D matter? Don't we already capture 3D images with normal cameras? And so the EVO 3D became a one-off.

Instead of revolutionizing the market, it appealed to a small consumer base, bringing in initial interest but falling flat when those consumers could find no real advantage and a larger consumer pool didn't realize the benefit.

Huawei did something similar with its P9 release advertisements, where the tagline read:

> *Delivers photos with outstanding*
> *clarity, color and contrast.*

While the slogan offers consumers clear benefits in photo taking, it does so with technical language. The terms "clarity," "color," and "contrast" are all technical terms associated with photography. Sure, you may think that these are common terms, words that the majority of people would understand, but they're not. The language is technical and relates to the specification and capabilities of the camera, as opposed to the experience of the consumer. The tagline "Delivers beautiful photos" provides the same benefit without the use of technical language.

The issue with Huawei's slogan is that its technical grounding made it hard for the average consumer to relate, thereby making it almost impossible for it to resonate. The majority of camera phone users will set their camera to automatic and ignore specific clarity, contrast, and color settings. Just like with speed and web hosting, consumers expect image clarity, color, and contrast on camera phones to "just work."

So there is another level of consideration beyond just feature vs benefit. Huawei communicated the benefits of its product, but it did so in a way that failed to capture that market. The piece that was missing was resonance. Benefits can be communicated to consumers, but when they are done in a way that relies on the technical underpinning of a product, they often fail to resonate with the majority of consumers.

When Apple released the iPhone 7 later that same year, its slogan approached the dual camera smartphone from a different angle. It cut back on features and instead focused on what the product and the brand meant for consumers.

Evolution in every dimension.

Yes, there are two big words there. But you know what isn't there? Technical language. The slogan speaks to an experience, one that aligns with Apple's emotional goal and that provides a clear and resonant benefit for the consumer. In the mind of a consumer, they're getting their hands on an evolution in every dimension. It's not just that the camera setup has better contrast or clarity, or that it's capable of taking 3D images, or even that it can deliver beautiful photos. What Apple is saying is that every aspect of this device is just better than what came before. In other words, the benefit of this new device is universal.

The small web hosting company did the same. They simplified their language, made it accessible to everyone, and therefore allowed it to resonate. Instead of just reframing faster setup times as the benefit "get started faster," they adopted a larger, experience-driven rhetoric: Hosting that makes business easier.

And in doing so, they saw conversions increase significantly.

Building to Inspiration

Being able to inspire consumers is something almost all brands strive towards. It means that consumers will take actions beyond those they would with other brands. It means they will show you loyalty.

Apple inspires its consumer base, drawing divisions between those who fiercely defend the tech brand and those who would rather opt for Android. Coca-Cola also inspires loyalty, especially when pitted against its sweeter counterpart, Pepsi.

That inspiration doesn't come from nowhere. Rather, it is built upon a strong foundation of relatable, resonant, and communicative content. It is this that the brand pyramid represents.[7]

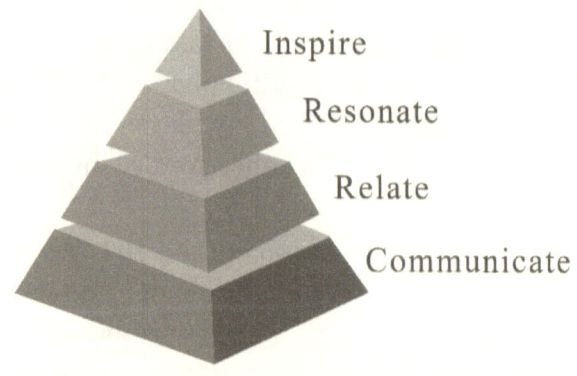

The Brand Pyramid

The brand pyramid serves two primary functions. One, it acts as a checklist to ensure that the message your brand's content communicates is effective. Two, it allows you to measure the power of that content on a simple scale.

Let's take Nike's "Just do it" line as an example. Does it communicate meaning? Yes, it communicates the notion that people can just do what they want to. Does it resonate with their consumer base? Yes, it speaks to the human desire to move forward. Is it relatable? Anyone who has experienced hiccups in life should find it relatable. And finally, most importantly, does it inspire? If it fits the three categories below, chances are it is capable of inspiring. As we know from Nike's market dominance, it does, indeed, inspire.

While it's important to build a story with your brand, it's also important to consider how that story can be applied to the brand pyramid. If the story doesn't communicate effectively, then it won't provide your consumers with the information they need to make a purchase. If it's not relatable, then consumers won't be able to place themselves into the role of the protagonist. And if it doesn't resonate effectively, then it won't be enticing enough. Finally, if you miss one of those areas, then it's very unlikely your brand's stories will be able to inspire action and loyalty.

Part 3

Shift

Enter the conversation already taking place in your prospect's head.

- Robert Collier

Introduction

In the final section of this book, I am going to introduce Shift. Shift is both an idea and a practice. It is the idea that language can be used to motivate brand distinction in an industry, and it is the practice of making that distinction a reality.

Throughout history, brands have made themselves distinct. Coca-Cola has become a megalith of the beverage industry, Nike a champion of sports apparel, and De Beers a cartel for diamonds. Every brand I have mentioned in this book has made itself distinct from the other brands in its industry, to the point that they have become mythologized. They have done this by finding the "secret sauce" and resonating with their audience: truly resonating.

For years, only the largest and most successful businesses have been able to do this by combining a mixture of expert psychology, expensive research, and clever creatives. But modern technology has meant marketers are no longer required to pay expensive consultation fees. You already have, at your fingertips, more data than you could ever hope to use. You just need to know how to use it.

The goal of Shift is to take what audiences expect of a brand and an industry and use it to inform marketing that fuels action and decision-making processes. It's a strategy that uses the wealth of information already available to inform language and messaging so that it resonates, informs, and inspires. To do this, language is placed on a spectrum.

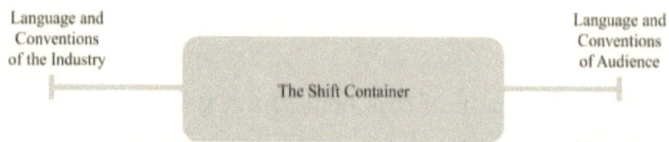

Shift places language into a spectrum.

In one direction is the language and conventions of the industry. This is how audiences expect brands within an industry to behave and speak to them. For example, we talked about how tech brands limit their use of adjectives while travel brands include them as often as possible. Brands cannot move outside of these expectations too quickly or they create feelings of uncertainty and discomfort. When trying something new, the first thing you need to know is what these boundaries are.

In the other direction is the language and conventions of the audience. These are the beliefs and aspirations of the consumers who buy from a brand; they are also what brands need to resonate. The goal is for brands to move from leaning heavily on industry language to a place where they're able to distinguish themselves and resonate through audience language. The Shift Container is a way to do this.

As a marketer, it is your job to find ways to make your brand one that people want to buy from. It's your job to mythologize the business you work for, turning it into a brand that doesn't just outsell the competition but outranks it. The Shift Container is a tool for doing this by creating clear linguistic clusters (or segments) that target and realign a brand with audience language, while also paying attention to limitations set by the industry. To do this, we'll need to explore why this theory works and how each part fits into the larger whole.

This final section of *The Language of Brands* will begin by looking at how language can be analyzed, including some of the core terminology in linguistics. It will then look at what a brand is. It will explore a brand's role in marketing and uncover some of the psychological mechanisms that underlie a brand's ability to sell. We will then change tack and explore the language of industry. This will be done through a look at search engine optimization (SEO), including its history, how Google's search algorithm works, and how you can use that knowledge to create content that ranks highly. This will be followed by a look at audiences and how to find and measure their expectations from a social and discourse perspective.

Finally, we will address the idea of Shift. We will begin by presenting a model for Shift, including the relationship between the language of an industry and the language of an audience. We will then highlight where Shift sits on a spectrum of language, and how it can be found.

Once you've finished reading this book, you should be equipped with the tools you need to begin finding and driving Shift in your organization. So, if you're ready to begin...

7

Picking Apart Language

According to Microsoft, the average human has an attention span of 8 seconds. [1] So it's no surprise that when marketers are asked to look at competitors and their content, they draw quick assumptions about what kind of language is being used. Unfortunately, time and time again, these assumptions prove to be incorrect and unrepresentative of the content as a whole. But isn't this OK? In a world where attention lasts just 8 seconds, what's wrong with noticing only some linguistic features and dismissing others?

The problem is that, according to Sabine Kastner, a professor of psychology at the Princeton Neuroscience Institute, what we pay attention to is subjective. "Perception is discontinuous, going rhythmically through short time windows when we can perceive more or less." [2] For most people looking quickly at a brand, the most salient elements are going to be the ones they resonate most strongly with—or that provide evidence for conclusions they've already drawn. As marketers, we need to pull ourselves away from this approach and see our brands impartially. It's vital that, instead of being drawn into our own marketing myths, we pull ourselves away and approach them from unbiased perspectives. When marketers don't do this, even the biggest of brands can fail.

In 2004, Dove launched the critically and publicly acclaimed "Real Beauty" campaign. Consisting of advertisements, workshops, videos, and events, it saw Dove's profits soar by over $1.5 billion. The campaign was a huge success for the marketing minds behind Dove. Not only did it resonate with Dove's audience, it also set the stage for all of Dove's marketing campaigns for almost fifteen years. They probably could have kept going too, if they hadn't fallen victim to their own hubris.

Almost fifteen years later, Dove came up with the idea of Real Beauty bottles. These bottles were designed to reflect the diverse shapes of women. Some were tall and thin, others were short and round, some fell in between. There were six bottle sizes in total, each designed to "evoke the shapes, sizes, curves, and edges that combine to make every woman their very own limited edition." The reaction? As one customer said, "The Dove bottle with my body type hurts my feelings."

Images are not language. But as we discussed earlier, they communicate with us in the same way. The ways we interpret them originate in our understanding of social and discourse conventions. When it comes to packaging, discourse conventions tell us that shape reflects what is inside. Think about the products you purchase and what their packaging tells you. Tech products come in specific boxes—laptop packaging is, for example, almost always the same. Beauty products are no different. Ask any marketer in charge of beauty products and they'll tell you the same thing. The packaging is as important as any other touchpoint.

Unfortunately, Dove's new packaging missed the mark, and it did so for a very clear reason. When working with the same content in the same industry for an extended period of time, it's easy to forget some of the foundational principles that brought about that content. Instead of taking a step back and looking at the branding and its methodology as a whole, the marketers behind Dove's Real Beauty campaign paid attention only to the areas they found success in earlier: the diversity of women and their body shapes. If they had been looking at the packaging from the perspective of a customer, they would probably have seen why it was a problem almost immediately. But they didn't, and after fifteen years of campaigns built on the success of one, they had to find a new platform to build on.

For marketers using language, it's important to pay attention to campaigns and brands as a whole. This means taking a step back, analyzing the data, and then using that information to motivate more qualitative research and creative processes. For Shift, this means being able to analyze language data in large quantities with a clear and unbiased method. This is what is known as corpus linguistics. [4]

This chapter provides a quick introduction to some basic analytical linguistics terminology, along with how each can be used to show wider implications.

Corpus Analysis

At the core of this book's methodology lies corpus linguistics. While too large a field to cover in detail here, corpus linguistics is the process of taking large quantities of texts and putting them into a tool for the analysis of high-level similarities and differences.

Often, these corpora are digital text files made up of content from a variety of different sources. However, the content in a single corpus often revolves around a single point of research. For instance, you may have one corpus that collects all social content, another that collects web copy, and another that collects ad content. Alternatively, you may have one corpus that contains content from one persona, while another takes content from another.

Corpus creation can be a complex task and involves a range of different skills and techniques. I will not go into depth as to how to create the best corpus in this book—that information could inspire another volume. However, in general, you want to make sure that you avoid collecting content that you don't want to analyze. This includes menu text, footer text, and any meta information that isn't viewable by consumers (unless you're creating a corpus for SEO).

Modern technology has also added some exciting features for corpus analysis, including image markup. This allows marketers to now take large numbers of images and then analyze them for specific features they define. This may be color, objects, "busyness", or something else. Images are just another form of language, and so the principles outlined in Shift can also be applied here.

As I explain Shift, I will use the word "corpus" many times. If you aim to engage in Shift yourself, this means that you will have to collect content from multiple sources and place it into a single text file. This would then be put into a concordancer tool that offers the functionality mentioned below: frequency, word class identification, syntax breakdown, and collocation.

Tokens

When you read a text, you read one word followed by another. Each evolves your understanding of what the text is about, how its narrative changes, and whether you identify with it or not. As a result, the power of individual words can be enormous. When conducting linguistic research, these individual units are not called words; they are called tokens. Let's take a look at an example by analyzing a common sentence.

The quick brown fox jumps over the lazy dog

You've probably seen the sentence above before. [5] In fact, you probably remember writing it during handwriting courses as a child. The phrase is what we call a pangram—a sentence that contains all the letters of the alphabet. It is as good as any sentence for understanding what a marketing linguist sees when they look at a text.

In linguistic speak, tokens are defined as "a thing serving as a visible or tangible representation of a fact, quality, feeling, etc." Much as we discussed in the understanding language section, words are not innate bearers of meaning, but vessels through which our understanding of the world is funneled. Our concept of a fox does not come from the word fox, but from the education we received as children. As such, tokens are the primary tool for the manipulation of a text and its social and discourse conventions.

In the sentence above, we have nine tokens, all of them different from one another, yet each just as important to the meaning of the sentence as the one before. Each helps to shape and mold in our minds what is happening in the sentence, from the nouns fox and dog, which define the characters, to the verb jumps, which tells us the main action of the story.

We could easily change what's happening in the story by changing any one of the tokens in play. Each change would do more than just the obvious. If we change the token dog to elephant, for example, we aren't just changing the character of the dog; we're also changing the capabilities of the fox. After all, a fox that can jump over an elephant is surely a lot more athletic than one that can jump over a dog.

Even the token the plays a vital role in our understanding of the text. Determiners exist in English for a reason. In fact, most languages include some form of determiner. Even Chinese, with its context-heavy grammar, will draw a distinction between a and the. The dog refers to a specific dog; a dog could be any dog. As texts are built out, these determiners can play a vital role in the creation and positioning of social actors and products. The product for you is very different from a product for you.

Word Classes

In the sentence The quick brown fox jumps over the lazy dog, what different word classes can you see? If we were to break it down and list them out, we would see something that looks like this:

> Nouns: Fox, Dog
> Adjectives: Quick, Brown, Lazy
> Verbs: Jumps
> Adverbs: Over
> Determiner: The

Each of these different word classes has its own role within the text. Determiners clarify nouns, and nouns tell us about characters. Adjectives then help us to paint a more vivid picture of those characters, verbs share their actions, and adverbs let us understand more about what those actions involve.

Nouns and verbs are often the most significant for marketers looking to define their tone and style. [8] Nouns have the power to create unique characters and entities within a text, while verbs let them inspire action, move marketing stories, and more. It's not surprising that Plato, one of the first Western figures to consider the parts of language, said that sentences are "a combination of verbs [rhêma] and nouns [ónoma]." He didn't even consider the role of adjectives and adverbs in language.

Remember, nouns are not always the placeholders of characters. They can also provide context by providing the name of a setting, an event, or an association. Because of their nature, nouns tend to bring with them a finite attribute to a text and its meaning. In the Nike slogan "Just Do It", there are no nouns. There is the pronoun it. But it isn't the character of the text. It doesn't even have a clear meaning: it could be anything. Instead, Nike's omission of a noun is intentional and is something we will look at again later.

A brand's tone and style are often defined by the types and frequency of word classes it uses. Modern tech brands, for instance, have a tendency to stay away from adjectives. Amazon Web Services makes very little use of adjectives in its marketing material. The header on its homepage isn't some fancy line of prose. Rather, it just states "Start Building on AWS Today."

In other industries, such as travel, adjectives have become so ingrained in marketing material that we just assume they will be there. They have entirely become a part of that industry's discourse conventions. Phrases like "top deals", "best destinations", and "special offers" are commonplace, using adjectives in phrasal units that can easily be found using collocates—something else we'll revisit in a moment.

Adverbs, similarly, are rarely used. Except, unlike adjectives, this has become the case in most industries, not only some. This has largely come from a belief in the copywriting world that readers prefer content that speaks directly and succinctly to them, and a lot of writers believe that adverbs get in the way of this.

As a result, verbs are a powerful tool that marketers often feel they need only use in their unmodified state. They form the basis of emotionally resonant calls to action, with the right verb aligning itself with the idealized experience of the customer. And remember what neuroscientist Antonio Damasio found: emotion is key to the decision-making process.

Frequency

When considering the role of tokens, we have to first consider their frequency. How often does a particular token occur within a text? What does that mean for the text as a whole, and what does it tell us about tone and style?

Frequency is a powerful tool for drawing quantitative hypotheses from large samples of texts. [6] If you were to perform a linguistic branding exercise (something we'll cover later in this book), frequency would underpin a lot of your initial research. The more a word features, the more it has been purposefully chosen over alternatives. W. Ross Winterowd wrote that "The main factor in tone is [...] the words that the writer chooses." Frequency is a clear indication of the type of tone a brand is trying to create across its content.

Let us take a look at the book *Alice in Wonderland* by Lewis Carroll. This novel has over 27,000 tokens from start to finish. That means it has over 27,000 words. The most frequent token is the. The, as we already discussed, is a determiner. Determiners appear in line with nouns to connote a specific object, thing, or person, as opposed to a generic one. As a result, you can expect determiners to have high volume in character- and product-driven stories and texts.

Rank	Frequency	Token
1	1642	the
2	872	and
3	729	to
4	632	a
5	595	it
6	553	she
7	545	i
8	514	of
9	462	said
10	411	you
11	397	alice

The top 11 tokens in Alice in Wonderland.

Then there are the pronouns. These are tokens like "you", "she", and "I". Pronouns can tell us a lot about a text and its tone and style. The different pronouns used by an author let us know how they speak to their audience and connect with them. Copywriters are often told to use the pronoun "you" frequently in their writing. It means your writing connects with your audience, or so they say. As with Nike, this isn't always the case. It's very possible to include the audience without even mentioning them in the text. The mind is far more creative than we often give it credit for.

In a study of attention, researcher Kalina Christoff and her team found results that they believed supported the hypothesis that—even while engaged in activities that require a person's full attention—the mind would wander as a way to enable creative thought associated with that task. This would even occur if that creative thought undermined immediate goals.[7] In other words, as we commit to attention-intensive tasks, our minds will wander down a rabbit hole of thought, filling in the gaps with assumptions. What this means is that, just like the marketing executives at Dove who saw their Real Beauty bottle designs only in terms of the success of their Real Beauty campaign, readers will often make assumptions based on what they expect to be there. The existence of characters is often assumed. When they are not represented formally, they are easily imagined.

Continuing to look at frequency, below pronouns we begin to find adverbs and adjectives like down and little. These describe nouns and actions and help to fuel our understanding of the text as a whole. Directional adverbs such as down are specifically important.

Finally, nouns will start to appear in the analysis. Depending on the type of text, nouns are most likely more infrequent than any other word classes found in a frequency analysis.

When looking at frequency, remember that it is only a high-level analysis of content and style. It should never be used in isolation, and instead should be used with some of the techniques mentioned in this section.

Syntax

Syntax is a set of rules and principles that govern the structure of sentences. In simple terms, this is what we call word order. Word order is a funny thing. Linguists throughout time have had theories as to why we choose the word orders we do.

In 1965, Noam Chomsky pioneered the concept of Universal Grammar, a theory which stated that there exists a genetically hard-coded universal grammar in all humans.[9] One that means any individual who grows up in a normal environment will adopt a specific syntax; e.g., distinguishing verbs from nouns and function words from content words.

Chomsky's theory of Universal Grammar has often been debated, with some linguists going so far as to call it pseudoscience. Wolfram Hinzen stated that not only does the concept of a universal grammar not align with accepted neo-Darwinian evolutionary principles, but also points out that there are no linguistic universals. In fact, if you look far and wide enough, you can find languages that are entirely dissimilar from one another.

Think about the De Beers line "A Diamond Is Forever." Both short and grammatically incorrect, the sentence defies the notion of a universal grammar. According to

Chomsky's theory, at least to some degree, readers should have felt a degree of uncertainty regarding its meaning. And as neuroscientists David Rock and Al Ringleb said in the first section of this book, uncertainty registers with the brain much like an error. But readers didn't; Gerety's line instead grew to become the line of the century, not stifled by grammar rules held by the few, but understood and adopted by the many.

The fact that Gerety's line could be adopted so easily shows that syntax is not necessarily universal, but instead flexible. Gerety's line was able to be successful because its syntax was adopted and assimilated by audiences as a discourse convention they could accept.

Assuming that syntax and word order are rooted in discourse conventions, we can then start to assign deeper meaning to words and their positions. Take, for example, nouns. Nouns are vital to sentence structure, and in many sentences, there are two. One is the subject; another is the object. In the sentence The quick brown fox jumps over the lazy dog, the fox is the subject while the dog is the object. The fox is doing the jumping, and the dog is being jumped over. Agency is given to the fox, and not to the dog.

The positioning of the nouns (the characters) is a clear indicator of not only power in the text, but also the characters' relationship to the reader. The fox, being the doer, is essentially whose perspective we take; whose actions we are meant to be aligned with. The dog, however, is just a secondary character. He literally has nothing to do but lie there.

In Nike's slogan "Just Do It", the subject isn't present. The character isn't there. It is because of this that we can become that character; we, the reader, can become the subject of that sentence, with the object becoming whatever we want it to be. The same is true of "A Diamond Is Forever." The diamond may be the subject, but it is not a character. The character is us, the reader, the owner of the diamond. Omission is not exclusion. Syntax being a product of discourse convention allows for this.

Clusters and Collocates

Looking at tokens is valuable, as is looking at concordance lines, but what if you're dealing with an amount of text too large to properly inspect a significant number of concordance lines? What if you're looking at multiple texts that use the same tokens in several different ways? This is where clusters and collocates come in.

Clusters and collocates are tokens that co-occur with a token you define. They provide more insight into a word by organizing these co-occurrences based on frequency and distance. Clusters primarily look at frequency around a specific token, while collocates look at frequency around a specific token when compared with frequency around other tokens.

For example, let's take a look at the token "down" in *Alice in Wonderland*. Sticking it into a cluster analysis, we are provided with the most frequent co-occurrences in the text. At the top of that list is "down the", with a total of 9 occurrences. Below this is "down on", with 7 occurrences.

By taking a look at the concordance lines for both of these terms, we can see that both have their own meanings and contexts. "Down on" references sitting, while "down the" is more frequent and references the famous "down the rabbit hole" line of *Alice in Wonderland*.

However, the tokens "the" and "on" are both very frequent throughout the entire text. As a result, they co-occur frequently with other tokens, perhaps even more frequently.

Collocates are the answer to this. By comparing these co-occurrences with other co-occurrences, it's possible to get a much clearer picture of when a specific token holds a significant relationship with another.

Looking at the token "down" and searching for significant collocates in *Alice in Wonderland*, we are shown a very different picture. Relevant collocates include "wrote" and "settled", both of which describe actions and allow us a slightly more detailed idea of what "down" means in the context of *Alice in Wonderland*.

As you conduct your own linguistic analyses, it's important to remember that language never works in isolation. As I've already discussed throughout this book, language relies on a wealth of conventions and concepts that already exist in the mind of the reader. Linguistic analysis indicates what these are, but it doesn't provide the full picture. To do that, you'll need to go further into how language and brand work together.

8

Language and Brand

Throughout this book, I've talked about brands and their ability to influence consumer thought. I've shown various examples, including Coca-Cola, McDonald's, Apple, and more. I've even explored how brands create stories to sell their products. But I haven't actually covered what a brand is.

The Oxford English Dictionary defines branding as "The activity of giving a particular name and image to goods and services so that people will be attracted to them and want to buy them."[1] This is a good definition of how branding works, but it doesn't represent the true enormity of brand in business and creative terms. I much prefer the definition provided by Patrick Davis, that brand is "a single organizing idea, a higher-order construct that everything comes from and aligns with."[2] This statement gives weight to the true significance of brand as a concept. Not only does branding encourage people to purchase products or services, it also focuses how consumers understand and relate to the company behind them.

In modern marketing, successful brands do this incredibly adeptly. Branding is the reason that when we think of Nike, we think of limitless potential, that when we think of Coca-Cola, we think of a happy family Christmas, and that when we think of McDonald's, we think of American burgers. Brand is a concept that ties together the individual components of a product and forms them into a single, congruent whole that allows consumers to relate. Marketing is a by-product of brand. It is the process a company goes through to make brand real, tangible, and relevant; from a single line of text on print collateral to a long-form article published on a Tuesday. Brand is the jug that holds and shapes everything else. Marketing is what's inside.

When Umbricius Scaurus branded his fish sauce in the 1st century AD with the slogan "the flower of garum", he brought together the individual components of his product under the congruent whole of a brand. By doing this, he encouraged a simple belief structure around his product. No longer was it just fish sauce, it became "the flower of" fish sauce. Regardless of the real-life, tangible experiences of consumers, the brand was consumed by the myth. Consumers didn't buy Scaurus' fish sauce. Instead, they were buying the idea of what fish sauce could be. In other words, the quality of the product may have influenced the creation of the brand, but it was the brand—the myth—that caused the popularity of the product.

McDonald's has done the same. Whether we like it or not, the fast-food chain has become synonymous with the idea of the American burger; Nike synonymous with sports and potential; and Apple, with its unique marketing campaigns and products that challenge expectations, synonymous with innovation. Everything that these companies do serves to perpetuate their brand; to continue the idea and make it more concrete. And, in fact, a lot of these brands' detractors bring up that McDonald's isn't the perfect American burger, that Nike shoes aren't the best sports apparel, and that Apple is no longer the innovation powerhouse it once was.[3] Just like with Scaurus' fish sauce, the consumer experience isn't the most important; the brand is.

So, creating a brand that sells is not about providing the best product or experience. Products and experiences are precarious. For established businesses, there is always the possibility that something better will come along and take its place. For emerging businesses, it is hard to compete with competitors that have vast amounts of capital behind them. Instead, the best brands succeed by perpetuating their own myth, just like Scaurus did with his fish sauce, just like McDonald's does with its burgers, and just like Apple does with its technology.

When we think about how brands create and perpetuate their own myth, we must think in terms of convention. Not the social conventions of consumers, but the discourse conventions of the industry—the language of the industry. Once we do this, we can see that there is a clear difference between good and great brands. When good brands perpetuate their own myth, they align themselves with existing industry conventions. When great brands do it, they challenge them.

The Psychology Behind Branding

McDonald's had spent decades as the world's number one fast-food restaurant. At first, they created burgers faster than anyone else. When that was no longer unique to them, they sold the public on the idea of the American burger: *buying McDonald's meant buying into national pride.*

But by the early 2000s, McDonald's was in trouble. Stock prices for the fast-food giant were in freefall as sales of the American burger shrank. The problem? The brand's promise of the American burger no longer resonated with the mainstream public.

At some point after the turn of the millennium, sentiment towards fast food had shifted. It was now common knowledge that fast food led to weight and health problems.[4] Multiple documentaries had been created, and news reports were happening almost daily. Parents stopped considering fast-food restaurants as places they could take their kids after school or when they were in a rush. Instead, they opted to cook meals at home or find healthier alternatives. For the first time since the company was founded in 1940, there was a possibility that McDonald's would no longer be the fast-food mainstay it always had been.

The executives launched a competition for ad agencies: create a campaign that would revitalize the McDonald's brand. They were looking for an idea that would help them to secure the mainstream youth market. And the campaign that answered couldn't have been any better.

Before we get into that campaign, though, let's cover some marketing basics. Number one: identity is a vital part of branding. Numerous studies have shown that when consumers are able to identify with a brand, they are much more likely to purchase—not just once, but many times.[5] In one study, conducted by Jennifer Edson Escalas and James R. Bettman, participants were asked to provide information on their own beliefs. They were then shown advertisements from different brands and asked what they thought. When shown brands and advertisements that included concepts that reinforced their concepts of self, participants would react positively. When shown brands and advertisements that contradicted their sense of self, they would quickly dismiss them.[5] These concepts don't have to be complex. In many cases, they are as simple as "conservative," "hippy," or "athletic."

Take, for example, the De Beers advertisements. Each "A Diamond Is Forever" ad targets a specific audience. In most cases, that audience is young, 20-something females. De Beers advertisements, promoting the concepts of commitment, romance, and longevity, resonate with this audience. They would not, however, resonate with an eight-year-old, and we would probably see this manifest itself in their reaction (or lack thereof) to the advertisement. Similarly, a person opposed to the institution of marriage would likely react negatively to the campaign, dismissing the brand of De Beers outright.

But the psychology of branding doesn't stop with identity. It also needs to explain how we, as consumers, internalize those concepts and relate them to brand. To understand this, we have to first look at the way the human brain processes and retrieves information.

In his book, Daniel Kahneman talks about the difference between fast thinking and slow thinking.[6] Fast thinking is intuitive. It's the type of thinking we perform when we encounter an unexpected situation; when we're driving on ice and the car skids. Before we're even fully aware of the situation we're in, we react and turn the wheel. It's an instinctive type of thinking. The second type of thinking is more deliberate. It's the type of thinking we use when we're trying to calculate sums like 14 x 17.

When we first see brands, we use slow thinking. We connect the dots: the product, the design, the messaging. We create a picture of what the brand means to us, and how we either self-identify with it or don't. Once we've done this, the idea enters into a type of mental container—what I call the Shift container—that our fast-thinking brain can quickly retrieve. From then on, when we see something that triggers the brand, we recall that container and intuitively recognize it. However, in order for these containers to be successful, they have to remain simple. Too complex, and it's hard for the brain to neatly retrieve them.

This isn't the whole picture. While not necessarily part of our rational mind, containers only explain how we store and retrieve our knowledge of brands—not how we react to them.

Neuroscientist Antonio Damasio, who I previously discussed in relation to emotion and decision-making, also conducted a study into brands. Specifically, brand evaluation and emotion. Unsurprisingly, he found through fMRI scans that emotion isn't just a vital component in decision-making but also integral for brand evaluation, far surpassing information or facts.[7] These emotions, however, need to be based on something. That thing is the container.

Combining the work of Kahneman and Damasio, we can say that the container is the basis for our emotional reaction to brand: our emotional reactions are triggered and influenced by the information we collect during our initial and subsequent exposure to a brand—the same information that we store in the container.

In other words, the first time we see a brand, we collect information and build an easy-to-access container in our mind. When we then subsequently see that brand (in the form of a brand trigger), we retrieve that container and have an emotional response. This emotional response then reinforces existing ideas in the container.

Think all the way back to when I talked about Umbricius Scaurus, his fish sauce, and the slogan "the flower of garum". For the Romans who consumed his product and brand, their initial exposure to the fish sauce could have been through any one of a number of different touchpoints—including the slogan. However, every time they subsequently engaged with the slogan—even briefly—they would have reinforced the concept of pleasant-smelling fish sauce, causing the emotions of optimism and interest to reemerge, and the mental container of the Scaurus brand to strengthen.

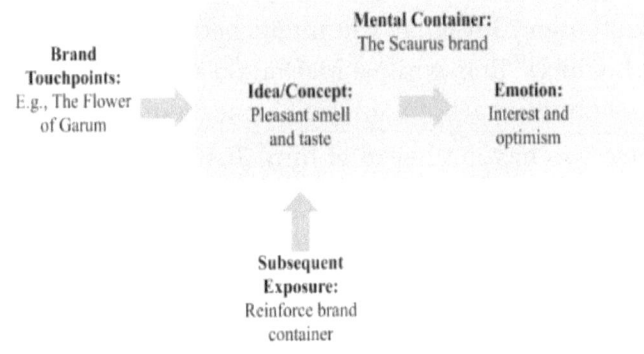

The mental container and brand exposure.

This is why branding is so important, especially during the initial stages of exposure. When done right, branding allows consumers to emotionally identify with a business. And by challenging industry conventions and realigning the brand around an audience's concepts of self, with the end goal of emotional resonance, it's possible to create a powerful container that sticks.

For McDonald's, regaining its market dominance meant more than just creating a great advertisement. For years, the brand had relied on being the "ultimate American burger". A great advertisement would only reinforce this concept. This was no longer what audiences wanted. Instead, McDonald's had to change who they were—not only the concept but also the container. They had to rebrand.

McDonald's first launched the "I'm Lovin' It" campaign in September 2003. It was the first time they launched a single message across multiple marketing channels at the same time. The brainchild of Heye & Partner, a relatively small marketing firm based in Germany, it would go on to become the company's longest-running ad campaign. But what you might not know is that the "I'm Lovin' It" line, while a McDonald's-branded slogan, was originally part of a Justin Timberlake song.

In case you haven't heard of him, Justin Timberlake is a famous American singer. He started out on the Disney show *The All-New Mickey Mouse Club* as a child, later joining the pop group NSYNC, and finally embarking on a solo career. By the time McDonald's approached him to sing "I'm Lovin' It" in 2003, he had already released his first solo album, *Justified*, which debuted at number two on the Billboard 200. To say that Timberlake was popular with a younger audience would be an understatement. He was a star. But when he first sang "I'm Lovin' It", it wasn't just a marketing gimmick.

Steve Stoute, the marketing executive who first introduced McDonald's to Timberlake, called the move reverse engineering. He believed that it was possible to boost the credibility of a brand by first "putting it in a pop-culture form that isn't connected in any way." He was right. The move boosted McDonald's credibility, but it also did something else. It changed the "American burger" container that consumers had attached to McDonald's for years. As consumers bought Timberlake's CDs and listened to his music, separate from the McDonald's campaign, they created a separate, distinct container that included the concepts of health, quality, and youth. Then, once McDonald's included the jingle as part of their marketing advertisements, those concepts were easily transposed to the McDonald's brand and container.

In other words, Timberlake released the song "I'm Lovin' It", and consumers heard the song and attached concepts associated with Timberlake to a mental container that could be easily retrieved. McDonald's then released their ad campaign. Consumers, recognizing the jingle from the Timberlake song, then retrieved their Timberlake container and associated it with McDonald's, bringing along the ideas of health, quality, and youth.

McDonald's still lives off the success of this campaign and continues to promote the "I'm Lovin' It" branding around the world. They now have over 37,500 stores worldwide, and each of them features its own version of the "I'm Lovin' It" slogan. In Germany, the country where the jingle originated, the phrase is "ich liebe es". In China it's 我就喜欢 (I just like). And in Egypt it's اكيد بحب (sure, I love).[8] Since their success in 2003, McDonald's has kept its branding consistent, with minor variations based on geographies.

Of course, other campaigns have come and gone as well, but "I'm Lovin' It" has remained a staple throughout. Most importantly, the slogan is no longer tied to Timberlake. Now the slogan has become so strong that it is able to perpetuate itself, much like Nike's "Just Do It" and De Beers' "A Diamond Is Forever". The fact that "I'm Lovin' It" comes from a song by Justin Timberlake, for which he was paid $6 million, is no longer common knowledge. Instead, his role in McDonald's 21st-century rebranding has faded into obscurity, and you're more likely to be asked about the song as part of an esoteric pub quiz than in any interaction with a teenager.

The Consistency of a Concept

Think back to neuroscientists David Rock and Al Ringleb, who said that uncertainty causes discomfort. A certain amount of discomfort works in favor of emerging brands, but it can be deadly for established ones. Consistency means certainty, which means security, comfort, and repeat business.

Consistency doesn't come from a slogan. The best brands show consistency in the concepts they inspire. Nike's true power is not in the slogan "Just Do It", but in the meaning behind that slogan: the concept of unlimited potential. Similarly, De Beers is not so influential because of the line "A Diamond Is Forever". While a powerful testament to the true value of a diamond, it simply cannot carry the same weight as the concepts of romance and commitment.

Brands inspire concepts. When they do so consistently, they inspire movement and action. And when those concepts align with the identity consumers have drawn for themselves, they not only become buyers, but advocates as well. Think back to the last time you were recommended a pair of Nikes or someone said they wanted to go to McDonald's instead of KFC. Those individuals are brand advocates. They are not only purchasing the products themselves but encouraging others to buy in as well.

In 1984, Apple leveraged the power of brand advocates when they released the first Macintosh commercial, a commercial that reinforced a single concept. The ad featured an unnamed heroine carrying a hammer, running through a dystopian society similar to the one in George Orwell's novel *Nineteen Eighty-Four*. She reaches a large room, where the masses have sat down to watch an orator on a large screen. She swings a hammer around, as though she is swinging a discus. Releasing it, the hammer strikes a screen and causes an explosion. Words appear on the screen: "On January 24th, Apple Computer will introduce Macintosh. And you'll see why 1984 won't be like "1984"."

The ad has since been described as a "watershed moment", mobilizing an entire generation of tech enthusiasts to pursue development and tech as a career path, and many companies to begin trying to outdo one another during the Super Bowl. It was an ad unlike any other that had come before it. It was unique and different. It was everything the Apple brand aimed to be, and it did exactly what it needed to do: it reinforced the concept that Apple is innovative.

Remember back to when we talked about tone and style and what Simon Sinek termed as Apple's why statement: "With everything we do, we aim to challenge the status quo. We aim to think differently." Apple's 1984 ad was a powerful testament to this. It resonated with a group of consumers that competitors had failed to properly reach, and in doing so it created a mental container so powerful that it continues to exist today. Some marketing experts even go so far as to say that Apple is its brand; that its success has little to do with its actual products, and everything to do with its ability to consistently and with great certainty push its audience towards recalling the concept of innovation.

Year after year, Apple pushes advertisements and content that build on this concept of innovation. The marketing lexicon focuses on language that draws connotations of the future and development. Every semiotic sign and symbol in play leads users towards this conclusion; from the futuristic nature of the clean, minimalist design to the innovative and unique designs of their products. As has been said before, "Apple is about imagination, design and innovation... It goes beyond commerce."

Lexicon of Brands

Concepts are the right start, but they can only take you so far. In order for brands to realize the concepts they inspire, they require language, whether that means written, spoken, or semiotic. It is here that lexicon comes into play. The lexicon of a brand is the language of a brand. It's the words that make up its core identity, and the signs and symbols that inspire certainty. A brand's lexicon should be easily recognizable and even easier to follow.

Take McDonald's and Apple, for example. These two brands have clearly distinct lexicons. Their websites clearly indicate as such. On Apple.com, you find words like "innovative" and "pro". Products stand in front of plain, monotone backgrounds. The text is simple, lacking adjectives or lengthy paragraphs. McDonald's, however, uses words like "quality" and "tasting". The images are colorful, and adjectives like "fresh" and "delicious" can be seen everywhere.

These differences go beyond industry differences. Even within the same industry, brands express themselves differently. This is because lexicon affects both style and tone. The language choices a brand makes, both in terms of written words and semiotic signs, lay the foundation for interpretation of a brand. Compare the two sentences below.

Life Tastes Good

Dare for More

How does each of the sentences make you feel? Think about the language that's being used, and what each is saying. The first line inspires a sense of relaxation: life is good, sit back and enjoy it. The second line, however, drives action. It drives you to challenge, to try, to dare. The two lines use different styles, and as a result, they have different tones. Considering this, which brand would you prefer? If you're more of a laid-back individual, you may feel that the first line appeals to you. If you're more competitive, the second line might.

In case you don't recognize them, the two lines above are marketing slogans from Coca-Cola and Pepsi, respectively. Both ran around the same time, between 2001 and 2003.[9] Now that you know which line belongs to which brand, and can compare the entire ecosystem of branding from each, would you change your preference?

Creating a core lexicon for your brand is the first step to keeping your brand consistent and your messaging intact. But remember, brand is "a single organizing idea, a higher-order construct that everything comes from and aligns with."

For Apple, that concept was always innovation. As a result, advertisements have always used language like "iOS7: The mobile OS from a whole new perspective," and "iPhone X Say hello to the future." The brand always talks about something new: a new way of seeing, a new way of doing, a new way of experiencing.

If we analyze copy from the Apple website, we see the same branding language extend throughout the site.[10] The token "new" is frequently mentioned throughout the copy, and some of the most frequent clusters are "never seen... before" and "like never before". The call to action "get more out of..." makes repeated appearances, going so far as to become a linguistic and navigational staple throughout the site. It's clear that as Apple has put together its content, they have paid specific attention to the language they use, not just textual, but visual as well.

The language a brand uses reinforces a consumer's ability to recall that brand quickly and effectively. By being able to do so, those consumers will quickly feel emotions that reinforce their concepts of self and that will increase their resonance with the brand.

Of course, concepts on their own do not encourage sales, just as language on its own does not encourage loyalty. But when language and concepts are brought together in simple models that allow consumers to easily and consistently recognize a brand, they form a powerful vehicle through which consumers make purchases and commit to journeys.

For most marketers, this is where the concept of branding stops. Much like Pavlovian conditioning, once the correct emotional response is acquired, marketing has done its job, and everyone goes home. But there's more to be done, and truly driving the resonance of a brand means understanding what emotional concepts resonate and the language behind them.

Powerful brands do more than just evoke concepts; they evoke aspirational concepts. Apple inspires consumers to strive towards innovation, De Beers inspires consumers to experience committed relationships, Nike inspires consumers to lead successful lives with no limits, and McDonald's inspires consumers to lead healthy, happy lives. Inspiration comes from looking to the future in some shape or form, and that is exactly what your brand and its language need to do, without exception.

9

Understanding Your Industry's Language

In the early 2010s, there was a small tech startup. It was a hurried project, cobbled together under the umbrella of a larger brand. Resources had been taken from wherever they could be, with the budget more a case of "use what you can get your hands on" than "this is your annual number". Already understaffed in the marketing and sales departments, this meant careful reallocation and strategy development. It also meant showing success quickly.

As time passed, the team grew impatient. Six months had gone by, and little had been seen by way of traffic, engagement, or revenue. At this point, a lot of time and money had been poured into the venture. The team had gotten approval for costly coupons and discounts for new clients, they had run advertisements in industry publications, and thrown a few thousand dollars at paid advertising. They had done everything they were meant to do to get a small, unknown brand off the ground. The problem was that none of it was actually working.

The response of leadership was to bring in another team member, one well-versed in marketing and content strategy. The team already knew what their problem was. They were unsure about their industry and their brand's position within it. After having conducted competitor research, they found that the ideas and concepts they believed should have resonated with their consumers were not. By leveraging a content expert, the idea was that they would be able to work on building the brand and then leverage the brand to increase revenue.

I was introduced to the brand almost a full year after it had first gone live. In a series of small-scale research studies, I found that leadership was correct. Not only had the brand failed to find content that resonated with their audience, they had invested in the wrong areas while trying to do so. The budget had disappeared into paid advertising campaigns, but little had been used to support or build an identity. No brand guidelines were present, no messaging had been agreed on, and when I went to visit the blog—a startup's core hub for organic brand building—all I found was a series of articles unrelated to one another, lacking a clear brand voice, and published sporadically. It was not surprising that the brand had failed to generate much traffic or revenue. Their strategy was inconsistent, lacked direction, and failed to connect with consumers. At the core of their problem was the lack of a clear and resonant content strategy.

This brand isn't an exception to the rule. By some estimates, as many as sixty percent of marketers don't have a documented content strategy. That's sixty percent of marketers creating content with little idea of where they are going.

I immediately set to work creating one. If I could create a clear pathway forward, then I would be able to not only promote the brand, but also increase reach, raise awareness, and drive sales. Unfortunately, the remaining budget meant a lot of traditional avenues were off the table. So instead of investing in expensive syndication programs or content creation agencies, the content that was decided on was going to have to be created in-house. With resources already stretched thin, we settled on a strategy that included carefully curated blog articles, an engagement- and traffic-driven social strategy, and the smallest amount of paid advertising. The posts were created, scheduled, and promoted.

Unfortunately, results didn't appear quickly enough; it can take months to build up enough value for a post to hit the first page. And just a month after the first round of marketing assets went live, the project was abandoned. While still maintained online, any hope for future development was dashed as resources were reallocated elsewhere.

A year later, I returned to the brand's analytics. I was curious. I wondered if my strategy and content had made a difference, or if the brand had instead faded into obscurity.

What I found was unexpected. Instead of losing visibility or remaining stagnant, the brand had grown. Organic traffic had jumped significantly. The site had gone from seeing just a few hundred users a month to several hundred thousand in the last year. Instead of twenty or thirty, the handful of articles that had been created were now seeing thousands of unique page views every month. And visitors were doing more than just viewing one; they were viewing multiple. They were engaging with the brand more than we could have ever hoped for. It was my first look at the true power of inbound SEO, and I was shocked.[1]

What happened isn't unique. This isn't the story of a brand that we saw doing well and then decided to revitalize. This is the story of a brand that began to thrive on its own by virtue of the way that Google and other search engines aim to optimize the search experience for users. The content that we had created was all relevant, informative, and structured, and it fit perfectly within what was expected in its industry. This included the language used in the articles and the creative employed as part of the paid and social strategy. The content ranked well and generated organic traffic because it resonated with what algorithms had learned about the industry. But just because it resonated with a machine does not necessarily mean that it resonated with consumers. This is an important distinction.

Industry language and audience language are two different things. Industry language—or convention—concerns itself with what an industry currently looks like. It's an amalgamation of the creative, guidelines, and messaging of all the brands within an industry. It indicates what consumers expect from that industry, and, as a result, what machine algorithms like Google expect. The content strategy aligned around the startup brand did this excellently. It targeted keywords that were expected within the industry, it promoted a brand message that resonated with Google's algorithm, and it aligned creative with what other brands in the space were doing.

On the other end of the spectrum lies audience language—or convention. This is instead concerned with what audiences actually want, outside of a brand and industry. Every individual has their own aspirational hopes and dreams. Audience language asks, if you could take a brand's audience and narrow those down to one single promise, what would that promise be? The tech startup didn't do this well, even after a new content strategy was implemented. We'll explore this in more detail later.

This chapter focuses on the former. It asks how marketers can easily identify and understand the structures and conventions that already exist within their industry. However, instead of using this information to inform an entire content strategy like with the tech startup, it positions this information as providing a platform from which to create a strategy that does more than resonate. The language of industry, when combined with the language of audience, can create a brand that distinguishes itself.

When McDonald's decided to rebrand in 2003 with its "I'm Lovin' It" campaign, it realigned its branding to meet the language of its audience, which happened to be embodied in the concepts of youth and vigor. The McDonald's team did this by coordinating their brand image with that of Justin Timberlake and pop music. However, throughout this process, they unmistakably maintained the identity of a brand that sat within the fast-food industry; they understood and maintained the language of their industry.

Not all brands manage to maintain the language of their industry when rebranding. And when they don't, it shows. This is especially concerning when you consider that ninety percent of businesses go through a rebranding process annually.[2]

In 2010, the GAP executive team was told that their existing brand strategy didn't resonate with a young, cool audience. Consultants said that it was too old-fashioned, that competitors had modernized, and that if they wanted to maintain their market position, they would have to change to keep up. As one of the few clothing outlets to have logged a sales drop in 2010, it didn't take much convincing for the brand to agree.

On October 6th, their new logo—spearheading a rebranding campaign—was released to the public. Marka Hansen, president of GAP North America, said, "We chose this design as it's more contemporary and current. It honors our heritage through the blue box while still taking it forward."

Gap's 2010 logo (left) and previous logo (right).

GAP's new logo ricocheted around the internet, finding itself drowned in almost universal criticism. Loyal customers threatened to stop shopping at the store, graphic designers threw in their two cents on why the design was wrong, and GAP's share price dropped thirteen percent. One critic went so far as to say that it was "the worst logo ever".[3]

GAP's new logo was received so poorly because it didn't match the language of the industry or of the brand. GAP, having been founded in 1969, is what's known as a timeless brand, meaning that consumers don't expect it to change or disappear. It's also a fashion brand, and the visual language of fashion brands tends to include simple, clear logos that can be shown on clothes easily. GAP's new logo went against these conventions. One critic even went so far as to say it looked like "some failed low-fare spinoff of a major airline." What could be more exemplary of a brand's failure to adhere to industry expectations than someone saying it looked like it belonged in another industry?

GAP's mistake provides us with insight into what marketers need to pay attention to when making changes and adjustments to their brand. There are very real limitations to any rebranding strategy that a marketer spearheads. Understanding what consumers are looking for is one thing. It's another entirely to be able to understand how they expect that to be presented to them. It is no longer enough to just create content and expect audiences to digest it. Now, brands need to make calculated changes based on what consumers expect from their industry. This is not to say that these expectations do not change; they can (and do under the Shift model), but they must also be managed carefully in order for brands to remain resonant.

This chapter looks at the language of an industry (industry semantics) as a foundation for creating Shift. [4] It positions industry language and conventions not as something to duplicate, but as tools to motivate decisions and strategies that better resonate with your audience. In other words, instead of competitor and industry analysis being the be-all and end-all of the marketing discussion, it's the beginning; a tool capable of indicating clear guidelines within which a brand can play.

Luckily, one of the easiest ways to identify the language of an industry is by using a tool you probably use every day. It's something people carry in their pockets, as well as leave on their desks. It already includes information on all the other brands within your industry, and it ranks them depending on their ability to resonate with the expectations of that industry. What I'm talking about, of course, is Google.

Understanding SEO

Larry Page and Sergey Brin met in 1995. At the time, digital search was still in its infancy and lacked a lot of the finesse we have now come to expect. Pages were ranked based solely on how often a keyword would appear. This meant that a page featuring the word "buy iPhone" 1,000 times, without any ability to buy an iPhone, would rank higher than the official Apple iPhone page.

This is what is called keyword stuffing, and it's a serious problem for search engines because it can easily be "hacked" to stop them from returning relevant results. Instead, user queries would be met with results that included the most instances of that query. This meant researchers were unable to find the best articles to reference, consumers were unable to find the right product to purchase, and everyone else was delivered advertisements and spam. Needless to say, a search engine that doesn't deliver relevant results is, in a word, useless.

For years, developers tried to come up with ways to make search systems "unhackable" and easy to maintain. Most of the time, these efforts meant manual intervention from search engine team members to block irrelevant pages and websites from search altogether. Originally, while difficult, this was possible. There were just 23,500 websites in circulation in June 1995. Today, however, there are more than 1.5 billion websites and more than 40,000 search queries every second through Google, making manual intervention impossible. Predicting that the internet would grow to become what it has today, Page and Brin thought they had the answer.

They believed that the most important factor for determining rank had to come from people, as opposed to machines. Instead of focusing on the frequency of keywords, search engines needed to focus on the frequency of engagement from other sources. They developed PageRank, a system designed to rank pages based on the number of other pages that linked to them. In case you don't recognize why that sounds familiar, it's because it's the same methodology used in academic citation analysis.

The idea behind citation analysis is that the more an article or author has been cited by another, the more relevant and important that article or author must be. For instance, if an article about hunting for gold is cited by numerous other articles about hunting for gold, chances are that the original article is an authority on the subject. This works very well in the world of academia, where citations can be managed manually, but it becomes a problem when anyone can provide a citation. Marketers, growth hackers, and content farms can easily exploit this methodology to rank their content higher than others, even when it isn't the most relevant resource. This is because citations alone tend to self-perpetuate. As a source's citations increase, so too does the likelihood that it will be read by a larger audience. That larger audience, in turn, will provide more citations. By providing a "network" of citation sources, individuals could easily jumpstart this process by providing several of their own links and then allowing other sources to do the same. Over time, irrelevant content would eventually dominate results pages.

In the beginning, Google tried to fix this problem with technical updates. In 2003, the Florida update saw spam-friendly sites lose rankings just before the holiday. In 2005, Big Daddy changed how Google handled link canonicalization and redirects. In 2009,

Vince changed the algorithm to favor big brands over less well-known ones. And in 2010, MayDay saw long-tail queries increase in importance. Long tail, as the name implies, is traffic queries that are longer in form; queries like "1931 Coca Cola Print Ad" or "Walt Stack Sports Illustrated Article."

But Google continued to suffer from issues of keyword stuffing and irrelevant results. Each time they iterated on its algorithm, results improved, but only for a short period of time. Websites and content farms like eHow quickly managed to continue their march toward web domination, publishing almost one million items a month and ranking them. For comparison, Wikipedia was only producing a quarter of that in a whole year.

This wouldn't have been a problem if content farms churned out quality content that was addressing the needs of searchers. But it wasn't. Instead, it created "a race to the bottom situation, where anyone who spent time and effort on their content was pushed out of business." The inevitable result of quick, shoddy content creation meant that it paid less, and so content creators who had previously put in more time were forced to spend less time to compete. In a nutshell, quality suffered.

By 2012, Google realized that technical updates weren't going to solve the problem. In order to provide users with the best results, Google needed to judge relevancy on its own. Beyond citation analysis, it needed to be able to understand why people were linking to content and pages and transfer that knowledge into a system that machines could understand. Google changed the way it approached relevancy.

The first of these changes was to find a way for Google to understand the meaning of a token. Imagine never having come across the term Coca-Cola and then seeing the phrase "Coca-Cola." One of your first questions might be: does it refer to two separate things or one? From the perspective of a machine, "Coca" and "Cola" are two separate tokens. They don't have an innate link between them. In order to solve this problem, Google needed a tool to tell it what Coca-Cola meant. This came to be known as the Knowledge Graph.

Albert Einstein

Theoretical physicist

Albert Einstein was a German-born theoretical physicist who developed the theory of relativity, one of the two pillars of modern physics. His work is also known for its influence on the philosophy of science. Wikipedia

Born: March 14, 1879, Ulm, Germany

Died: April 18, 1955, Princeton Medical Center, NJ

Education: University of Zurich (1905), ETH Zürich (1896–1900), MORE

Spouse: Elsa Einstein (m. 1919–1936), Mileva Marić (m. 1903–1919)

Children: Eduard Einstein, Hans Albert Einstein, Lieserl Einstein

The Google Knowledge Graph in action.

The knowledge graph is essentially a knowledge base used by Google to enhance the results it delivers. It uses information taken from the public domain to help the search engine understand the meaning of different queries. For instance, if you were to search for "Obama's wife", the knowledge graph would tell Google that Obama's wife is Michelle Obama, and Google would instead run a search for her. Originally announced in late 2012, by 2016, it contained more than 70 billion facts.

Most of the time, when asked about the knowledge graph, SEO experts will state that it provides the information for the results section shown in the image above. However, the knowledge graph is much more complicated and important than this. In addition to providing a huge array of facts, it helps Google's search algorithm define what tokens actually mean. In other words, the knowledge graph is a tool for understanding semantics—the meaning of a word. Once a machine is capable of understanding the meaning of a word, it's much more capable of aligning that word and its meaning with a search query.

The knowledge graph was Google's first foray into natural language processing (NLP). It was a foundational tool for allowing it to understand the meaning behind what users were searching for, and thereby understand how to deliver relevant results. But it wasn't the full picture.

Natural language processing works by creating systems that help machines to understand and process human language. This can be incredibly complicated. While linguists have long been able to understand and interpret human language patterns and the reasoning behind them, computer systems are still catching up. This is because the way we communicate in real life doesn't follow a clear-cut set of rules. A comprehensive understanding of any one text, no matter how large or small, requires a deep understanding of language not only on a micro level (individual tokens and morphemes) but on a macro level as well. In other words, in order to truly understand what a text is talking about, search engines need to know what individual words on a page mean, as well as the meaning they create when combined.

In 2013, the Hummingbird update was released. Its aim was to ensure that "pages matching the meaning do better, rather than pages matching just a few words." Hummingbird made it possible for the search engine to connect different queries by placing a greater emphasis on the relationship between words. It did this by leveraging the power of the knowledge graph along with NLP rulesets. Context now played a vital role in the creation and ranking of content. It was here where search engines became a great resource for understanding and researching the language of an industry.

With the ability to contextualize words also came the ability to provide theme-based results. This meant that Google now went beyond synonyms to distinguish networks of language where the constituents all fell under the same concept. For instance, in an article about football, Google would expect to see the tokens "league", "teams", and "quarterback", as these are relevant contextual terms. This is known as the Latent Semantic Index (LSI), and is key to Google's ability to derive the language of an industry. [6]

Google has continued to update and iterate its search engine based on natural language processing, and in doing so has created a vast network of content, wherein each piece is assigned value for specific queries and topics. For most marketers, this network provides a guide for how to write individual articles and pages. But for the linguistic marketer and brand expert, it provides detailed information on expectations within an industry.

In the rest of this chapter, I will walk through how to identify the language of an industry. I will discuss how that language can be segmented, and how each of those segments can be used to motivate brands on the article level, the topic level, and a holistic level.

The Language of Industry

For most consumers, it takes five to seven impressions before they will remember a brand. As individuals, it takes time for us to internalize something new and unique. This is why so many marketers proliferate the idea that a distinct brand is so important: a distinct brand is memorable. It's key to securing consumer loyalty. In truth, however, the most memorable brands are rarely that distinct. In fact, if we look at branding as a practice, we begin to see similarities appear all over the place. Did you know, for example, that ninety percent of consumers expect to have a similar experience across different brands and channels, while one in three of the top one hundred brands worldwide use the color blue in their logo? The majority of brands are not unique.

Chances are that your brand isn't any better. While marketers and creatives have promoted the virtues of uniqueness, few brands have followed through. Instead, businesses have decided to go with what works, and it's not surprising why. Best practices have long been a motivating factor behind business decisions. They reflect what has worked for others in an industry, and they, all but certainly, indicate a strategy that will drive revenue.

The tech brand mentioned earlier is no exception. While every effort had been made to bring unique qualities to the brand's image and language, it had, ultimately, succumbed to best practices and competitor analysis.

The color scheme was a pastiche of other brands, the logo all but a duplicate of another. Reading each page, it was hard to tell that you were reading this brand specifically. You could have been looking at almost any one of its competitors. The only reason you knew it was different was because it had a different brand name plastered across it, with industry best practices laid out in a new, distinct combination.

Everything about that brand was taken from the language of the industry. The color scheme, copy, creative decisions, and messaging all came from what was already happening and working for other brands.

At the time, we thought what we were doing was incredible—that it was unique and distinct and would stand out in its industry for consumers. Instead, what we were doing was planting our stake in the ground, and we were trying to make it as clear as possible to everyone else, brands and consumers alike, what our stake was.

When we talk about the language of an industry, what we're really talking about is semantics. The Oxford English Dictionary defines semantics as "the meaning of words, phrases, or systems". While linguists often find themselves immersed in the words and phrases part, for marketers, it is the systems part that is most important. As an industry takes shape, it brings with it an entire language of textual and visual assets. These assets set the stage for new consumers and brands. They provide a cohesive ecosystem of expectations, from color to messaging to everything else associated with a brand.

In other words, when exploring semantics in relation to SEO, you shouldn't just be defining what a word or phrase means and then aligning that meaning to article and page keywords. Semantics are capable of providing something much more important. They can, with cleverly positioned research, provide you with a clear understanding of the conventions and expectations of an industry, so your brand can clearly define itself as a constituent and more.

For the linguistic marketer, the Knowledge Graph and Hummingbird update were probably two of the most significant updates ever made to Google. From this point onwards, marketers were given access to a vast network of conceptual language and ideas that fall under a single topic or industry.

Unfortunately, in most cases, marketers only use a fraction of the data available to them, or employ it in narrow frameworks. They will essentially "ask" Google what it determines to be ranking criteria for any one query. Similar content is looked at, word counts are taken into consideration, and LSI keywords are pulled. Each of these provides additional credibility to a piece of content by allowing it to align with Google's own algorithm for ranking. It is important information for improving SEO. But it's also an incredibly narrow view of the data and methodology behind Google's algorithm.

The information above, usually leveraged in traditional SEO techniques, can instead be turned into a clear map for charting how to navigate and distinguish a brand within a topic or industry. It can help highlight the expectations of an industry in terms of words, phrases, and systems. In turn, this provides marketers with the information they need to know to make their brand both exemplary of their industry and distinct.

To do this, the language of an industry has to be broken into three different tiers. Each tier targets a different level of language. This division can be seen in the diagram below.

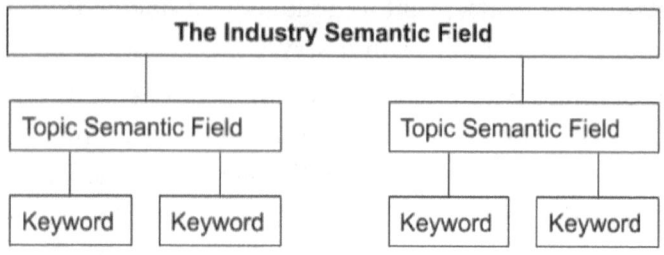

A method for creating relevant, resonant content with industry semantics.

Keywords

Keywords are words or phrases that help search engines to identify what a piece of content is about. They are the core language "ingredients" of a page.

There are two primary types of keywords. These are head keywords and long-tail keywords. The former tends to be shorter (sometimes single tokens) with higher search volume and difficulty. Head keywords are perfect for product and core pages. The latter tends to be longer phrases, with lower search volume and difficulty. These tend to work best for blog and promotional content.

For SEO, keywords have long been the key to creating content that ranks; from when frequency was the only ranking factor to now, where over 200 different signals are used by some search engines. However, they are most definitely not the only piece of the puzzle, and often, mid-level writers find themselves spending too much time conducting keyword research and not creating great content.

Keywords are usually found with keyword tools such as Google Keyword Planner. These tools provide information on volume and difficulty, among several other metrics, depending on the tool.

Topic Semantic Fields

Topic semantic fields, also known as the latent semantic index (LSI), are collections of language relevant to a particular conceptual field—often a core idea.

Most of the time, it is easier to find a core keyword for a specific topic and then use that to identify a relevant topic semantic field. Say your core keyword is "women's shoes". You could then create a corpus of page 1 search results and analyze the content for high-frequency tokens and phrases.

Often, there are multiple topic semantic fields in a single industry. Similarly, there are usually several different keywords that fall beneath a single topic semantic field. It's your job as a linguistic marketer to distinguish between high-value and low-value topics for your brand.

The Industry Semantic Field

The industry semantic field governs the content of an entire brand and provides a clear rationale for reader expectations. It does this by identifying high-level patterns seen throughout the industry across multiple topics and brands. An industry semantic field can be identified by creating a corpus of content created by other brands in your industry.

While not as important for creating high-ranking SEO content, the industry semantic field is an important governing framework for driving Shift. Not only does it provide clear guidelines specifying audience expectations, it also helps to pinpoint industry rhetoric that does not resonate.

To identify your industry's semantic field, you must conduct two different types of analyses. The first aims to create a lexicon—a list of tokens and phrases relevant to your specific industry. This helps to understand how an industry talks about subjects and topics. For example, in some industries, the consumer protagonist is highlighted explicitly with the pronoun token "you"; in others, they are only present as a result of inference, with the main pronoun used being "we". When conducting industry-wide analysis, results like this can be surprising but are an important part of understanding how your industry communicates with consumers.

The second analysis results in the creation of a tone and style guide. Tone and style are a vital part of industry expectations. For instance, tech brands avoid adjectives, while travel brands embrace them. The B2B agriculture industry looks to show impartial knowledge and functionality, while the investment industry focuses on the consumer and individual earning potential. Different industries, in general, accept and promote different tones and styles, and it is the marketer's job to identify these so as not to depart too radically from them.

Let's take the example of a fictional travel company called Asia Travel. Based in East Asia, this business has been offering low-cost accommodation to, largely, backpackers. It's not a huge company, but it does offer multiple locations in multiple countries, so it is established. The brand has had problems building brand momentum, with some of the internal team members feeling that the brand doesn't resonate with audience expectations of the industry. As a result, we perform a corpus analysis of the top brands in the backpacker travel industry. This provides us with the industry lexicon.

What we find is a long list of words and phrases that are used frequently. Some of the most frequent tokens include "to", "you", "with", "best", and "city". In a small-scale study, these five words are capable of telling us almost everything we need to know about the industry and its semantics.

"To" relates to journeys and traveling to somewhere. "You" tells us that the brand is consumer-centric—focusing on the consumer protagonist first. "With" refers to relationships and connections—visiting the park with family and friends or spending a day at the beach with friends. "Best" speaks to the brand's position on adjectives and the use of the superlative form. "City" tells us their destinations—a topic focus.

We can then use this analysis to better understand what language looks like on a macro scale. This enables us to define what the audience expects in terms of tone and style, providing us with the ability to create macro-rules for content creation.

Characteristic	Description
Personable	We focus on the customer; they are the protagonist; they make the experiences and go to places; we are their helper.
Adventurous	We focus on bringing unique experience to people's lives and making them excited.
Excessive	We don't settle for average. Experiences should be the best, the biggest, the greatest.
Convenient	We make things easy. From getting from point A to point B, to finding new experiences to chase.

Of course, we don't want to use this tone and style guide. This is not for our brand, but for us to understand how other brands in the industry communicate with consumers. This allows us to establish brand credibility by showing a knowledge of the wheelhouse we reside in, which in turn will be picked up by search engines and lead to content that ranks high.

As we work towards Shift as a process, we will also explore how an understanding of the language of an industry provides you with the knowledge you need to create distinguished brand experiences and strategies. It is your job to differentiate the semantics of your brand from those of another. However, at the same time, each piece of content that you create and publish should show cohesion and align with the language of your industry and the expectations of your audience. This is the power of Shift.

10

Understanding Your Audience's Language

The tech startup I mentioned in the previous chapter is a great example of how using the language of an industry can help marketers to grow brands and promote traffic. It speaks to the techniques that are needed to pull off such a stunt, and why doing so can help a brand become exemplary within its industry. Combined, they create a marketer's dream, a perfect storm of factors that combine to create distinction and follow best practices.

But the narrative starts to fall apart once you consider that the brand sat dormant for a year. Perhaps when I mentioned that previously, it struck you as odd. It certainly would have struck me as odd. How could the brand owners not have realized their business had grown? It's possible for a traffic increase to remain undetected over the course of a year, especially if the marketing team behind the brand weren't looking at the analytics. But for revenue growth to go undetected? At best, that's negligence. At worst, it's tax evasion. The reality was that it was neither. The reason it went undetected was because it hadn't grown.

While the tech startup had increased organic traffic substantially in a relatively small period of time, it hadn't seen more than an incremental rise in revenue. In fact, when we looked into the numbers in more detail, what we found was that our conversion rate was terrible. I had spent a month putting together a strategy that would increase traffic to the site. And it had done that. What I hadn't spent a month doing was considering how to turn that traffic into revenue.

The reason why it had increased traffic but not conversions was because the content was what search engines were looking for, but not what consumers were. Each of the articles we created ranked high in search results and brought in a substantial number of visitors. Unfortunately, they didn't provide enough of an emotional hook to draw those visitors to purchase. In other words, it perfectly complemented the language of the industry, but it almost completely dismissed language that connected with the audience: the language of an audience.

To test this idea, I went on to create another, alternate corpus based on the language used by the brand's audience. Unlike the original corpus created from website pages, blogs, and other promotional material from other brands, this second corpus was compiled using user-generated content.

User-generated content, as its name implies, is content that has been created by users. It includes, but is not limited to, content on wikis, social media platforms, forums, community sites, and individual blogs. In the modern, digital world, user-generated content is everywhere. Finding it isn't difficult. Finding the right content, however, can be.

The corpus I created looked to specifically target a single persona that I knew was traditionally a high-volume, high-value consumer in the industry. I broke out the corpus into the top 10 topics and tokens, and then I matched it up with the language I found in my initial analysis almost a year ago. What I found wasn't surprising and confirmed what I had suspected.

The language of the industry, identified a year ago, was largely different from the language of the audience identified in this new corpus. Yes, there was some crossover, but it was so minor when compared to the differences that it was obvious the brand had failed to resonate with consumers. It became clear that in order for a brand to succeed, it needs to strike a balance somewhere between the industry and the audience.

A few years later, in 2015, I consulted for a small business in the travel industry. They had recently seen a change in their industry where competitors were all talking about security in relation to travel. One of the people I spoke to went so far as to say it was "a paradigm shift in the industry."

The travel brand had realigned itself around this notion of security and had subsequently seen its revenue decrease. It wasn't by a significant amount, at first, but over six months, concern had built up amongst leadership around whether the direction they were going in was the right one. Did travelers really care about feeling safe when they visited new places? If so, what aspects of security, specifically, were consumers worried about?

Using the same system I had used for the tech startup, I conducted two corpus studies on the travel brand. One was to investigate the language of their industry—competitors, lexical fields, and voice. The other was to investigate the language of their audience—the way their consumers interact digitally inside and outside of their industry.

Sure enough, looking at the language of their industry, security featured as one of the most frequent topics. It wasn't the most frequent topic, but it was up there. Brands discussed, particularly, staying safe while traveling: avoiding getting sick, making sure your luggage isn't stolen, and finding trustworthy accommodation. Security was a popular topic, and, on the surface, it looked as though consumers were eating it up. Keyword volume was high for travel security-related terms, and article trackers seemed to indicate that consumers were visiting them. There was one problem: just like when I lined up the language of the industry and the language of the audience with the tech startup, the language didn't match.

Security was not one of the top 10 topics featured in the language of the audience corpus. It wasn't top 20 either, nor top 30. In fact, security didn't feature until I got through 50+ more popular topics. Security most definitely wasn't "a paradigm shift in the industry."

Instead, consumers appeared to be more interested in topics that revolved around discovery and exploration—almost the exact opposite of security in terms of concept and emotional resonance.

An explanation for why this is is that businesses like to play it safe. Instead of finding new and unique ways to market themselves, decision-makers often prefer to go with best practices and industry standards. By some accounts, as many as sixty percent of marketers are aware that they don't take enough risks when deploying new campaigns. Fear of failure and an inability to show potential for success are the building blocks of this impasse. Often, campaigns that begin with unique ideas are watered down until they mirror what is already present in the industry, under the guise of being best practices.

As it turned out, this is exactly what the travel brand had done. The reason security had become a staple of the industry's rhetoric was because another brand had promoted it as a point of distinction. While it hadn't fully resonated with consumers, it had drawn some initial interest. Over time, other brands picked it up, trying to offer the same experience as their competitor. Eventually, security became a talking point for almost every brand in the industry. The topic of security had become a part of the language of the industry, and other brands had followed it without thinking twice. Yet just like the content for the tech startup, while security may have become a staple amongst travel brands, it wasn't driving conversions. As a result, revenue suffered.

This chapter looks at the language of an audience as a second, key foundation for creating Shift. It positions audience language and conventions as a motivating force which, when used in conjunction with the language of an industry, can be used to create a brand that is both distinct and exemplary. It first discusses some of the principles behind the language of audience—from the role of emotion to its ability to transform the brand container. It then provides a series of different techniques for finding the language of an audience.

The Language of an Audience

The language of an audience does not come from nowhere. In 1900, a French tire company going by the name Michelin (you may have heard of them) created the Michelin Guide. At over 400 pages, the guide provided advice on hotels, eating establishments, and more. Brothers Édouard and André Michelin, the masterminds behind the guide, believed in its success so much that Michelin produced and distributed more than 35,000 copies for free. That was despite there being fewer than 3,000 cars on the road in 1900.[1]

Today, you probably recognize Michelin because of the Michelin star rating system, whereby a select number of restaurants and hotels are awarded one to three stars depending on their quality. One star means the establishment is very good and worth a visit if you are in the area, two means it is excellent and worth a detour, while three means the establishment is exceptional and worthy of a dedicated drive.

The Michelin brothers' idea behind the guide was simple: create a book that provided value to their audience. People crave new experiences, but often find themselves unsure of how to find them. The Michelin brothers offered a book that directed them not just to new experiences, but to new experiences that were exceptional. Just like McDonald's, Michelin went outside of their industry and explored the direct wants and needs of their audience. McDonald's did this by extending their marketing campaign to cover concepts associated with pop music. Michelin did it by exploring concepts associated with culinary adventure and the restaurant industry.

What Michelin and McDonald's both did was uncover the language of their audience and align it with the language of their industry. In other words, they looked at what their audience wanted—their desires, conventions, and concepts—and they used those to create content that truly resonated with their audience and that could help them build their brand.

If you pick up a copy of the original Michelin guide, released in 1900, you'll find, written in the preface: "This Guide was born with the century, and it will last every bit as long." Considering it's now 2020 and I'm writing about it here, that's more than accurate.

The tech startup mentioned previously could have taken a page out of the Michelin brothers' book. Not just in terms of creating an incredible piece of content that would perpetuate itself, but also in terms of listening to its audience. But what does that actually mean, to listen to the language of an audience?

The language of an audience is, simply, the language that a specific audience segment uses both when engaging inside and outside of a specific industry. In more complex terms, it's the conventions and concepts that specific audience segments attach to a product or service, or that they hold as being core to their identity.

For the Michelin brothers, it was the aspirational goal of exploration associated with drivers. It was the way they communicated with friends, relatives, and acquaintances about driving: the language they used in doing so and the foundational concepts and conventions those discussions were built on. For McDonald's, it was the concepts of youth and vigor. It was the other industries that their target audience interacted with and the way they interacted with those industries. For Coca-Cola, it was the family-associated concept of Christmas. It was what individuals really thought about Christmas, as opposed to depictions that already existed.

It's for this reason that the language of an audience is the motivating force behind Shift. While the language of industry functions as an anchoring force for ensuring expectations are met, the language of an audience functions as a driving force, ensuring the creation of empathetic journeys that resonate. In some cases, you may find that the language of industry and audience already overlap. But more often than not, it's likely that the language of your industry seeks to address problems with logical solutions, while the language of the audience seeks to provide answers to emotional ones.

In order to understand the significance of this, we need to revisit the psychology behind branding. There, we identified emotion as being key to the creation and reinforcement of brand "containers". We looked at some brands that chose certain language specifically because it would reinforce the emotional reactions that it did. Coca-Cola's Santa Claus was chosen to reinforce the emotion of happiness. Similarly, Nike chose Walt Stack because he would reinforce their emotional ideal of potential.

And it makes sense that brands would do this. As Antonio Damasio showed, emotion is a key component in the mechanisms that underlie decision-making. It helps individuals to take reasoned facts and attach emotional relevance to them: is this actually good or is it bad?

Emotion, then, is key to understanding the language of an audience. It is the unifying force of that language, ensuring it extends beyond just providing logical solutions.

In 1980, Robert Plutchik created the Wheel of Emotions. This diagram postulated different layers of emotion, all of which revolved around what he called the eight primary emotions of ecstasy, admiration, terror, amazement, grief, loathing, hate, and vigilance. For Plutchik, these emotions then divide out into secondary and tertiary dyads (feelings composed of two emotions). There have since been several different variations on the emotion diagram, but all have generally represented four main emotional counterpoints: happy, sad, afraid, and angry. [2]

This book is about creating distinction. It is about taking a brand above and beyond those that surround it and turning it into a paragon of its industry. To do this, we are primarily interested in only one of those emotions: happiness. This is because happiness builds advocacy and encourages consumers to share.

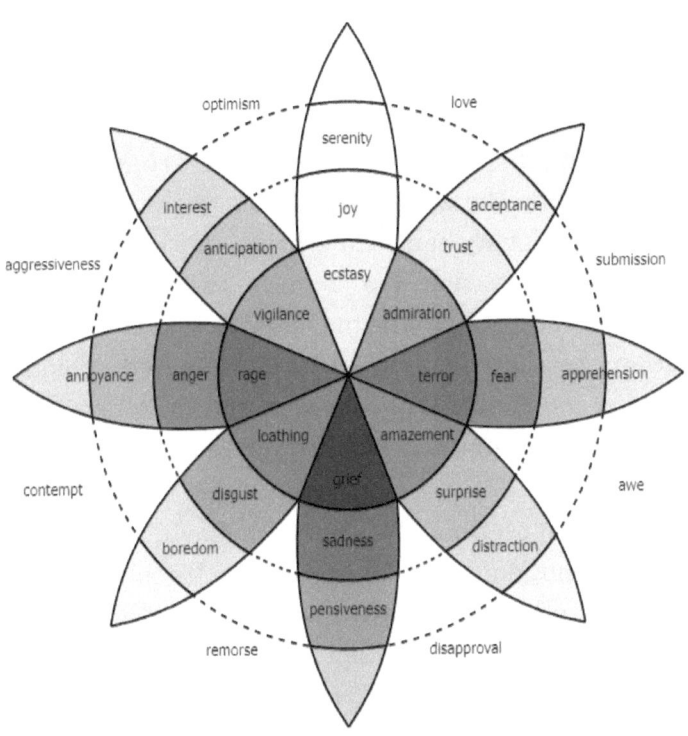

Plutchik's Wheel of Emotions.

In a study of over 7,000 articles published by The New York Times, Jonah Berger found that those shared more frequently showed a statistical leaning toward being positive in nature. Negative articles, while read and listened to, were not shared as often. [3] Why? Because we feel compelled to share happiness. One of the first actions we make in life is that of the social smile. The social smile is when a baby reacts to its mother's smile with one of its own. It is a powerful testament to how, wired into our left prefrontal cortex, is a desire to share the experiences we value and find joy in.

Happiness is key to creating incredible brands that are perpetuated by consumers. It is here where hope and aspiration exist. These two emotions are key for two reasons. One, because they result in happiness; the hope of achieving something brings with it a sense of pride and motivation. Two, because they are directed at the future. Similar to the marketing story mechanics of action vs satisfaction, future-orientated emotions provide consumers with the momentum to take action and achieve happiness. Not just once, but time and time again.

Think about McDonald's. Their "I'm Lovin' It" campaign was an emotional play for happiness. It took something that was otherwise disparate and unconnected to fast food—the idea of youth and vitality—and it made it a part of who they are. McDonald's became the fast-food choice of young people. It became aspirational, all while offering the convenient service it always had. Of course, the restaurant chain's marketing didn't resonate with everyone. Even today, large groups of middle-class individuals refuse to associate with the brand. But that doesn't matter because McDonald's was never targeting them. They never needed to understand their aspirations, or the language that would help inspire them. [4]

As you explore the language of your audience, you're looking for two main things. First, you're looking for discourse conventions. This includes anything related to how texts that your audience digests are created: what kind of language, formats, and imagery are used? These all provide vital information on the look and feel of your audience and who they are. For McDonald's, they found that their audience—young and mainstream—consumed texts that inspired the notion of health, youth, and sexiness. They replicated this in their marketing campaigns. Just go and watch a McDonald's advertisement.

The second piece you want to find is the social conventions that underlie those texts. What universal truths are believed to be true by that audience? What social structures are important to them? In many ways, social convention is more important than discourse convention. While discourse conventions provide an easily digestible setting, social conventions add the scenery. Without an understanding of the social conventions that a particular audience has, it's impossible to know how to truly resonate with them.

Segmenting an Audience

Among the first marketers to use data were Harlow Gale in 1895 and George B. Waldron in 1902.[5] Gale, a professor of psychology at Minnesota, began by sending questionnaires to find consumer opinions on campaigns. Waldron, a marketer, instead used tax registers, city directories, and census data to indicate the division of illiterate and educated consumers. While they used different methods, both set a precedent. By breaking audiences into different segments, each with their own desires, wishes, and optimal messaging, they were beginning to identify the roots of what, in this book, is referred to as the language of an audience.

Gale's technique was rooted in psychology. It attempted to view the inner workings of the consumer's mind and draw overarching conclusions. The problem with his research, however, was that it required consumers to provide him with data knowingly. It's well known that consumers, by and large, do not actually know what they want. As Henry Ford is said to have once said, "If I'd asked customers what they wanted, they would have told me, 'A faster horse!'" Gale's technique suffered from the context of his data and where it was taken from.

Waldron's technique, on the other hand, had the opposite problem. While it took data without the consumer knowing (or necessarily caring), it didn't provide enough insight into the consumer's mind. It lacked any real insight into how consumers thought. Instead, it relied on drawing largely stereotyped associations and assigning them to pre-identified segments based on class and geography. [6]

Needless to say, both Gale's and Waldron's techniques were missing something. However, they both pioneered the way for targeted marketing campaigns that truly resonated with audiences. Before them, the audiences that marketers targeted were created through a mix of assumptions and inferences. There was little room for change or segmentation, with a single, core strategy tending to take the lead in marketing proposals.

Today, marketers have access to an incredible amount of data for segmenting and understanding their audience. Demographics, geographies, benefit analysis, behavior, and more are all different areas that we can now explore to make informed decisions about who we target and how we target them. These allow us to paint a picture of our ideal audience and collect relevant, vital data that solves the problems with both Gale's and Waldron's techniques.

Robert Collier, a famous copywriter, once said that marketers have to "enter the conversation already taking place in your prospect's head." As early as the early 1900s, marketers were aware that it was the language of an audience upon which a brand's ability to sell was built. The Coca-Cola marketing team knew it when they targeted families with their campaigns. Nike knew it when they targeted athletes with the promise of unfulfilled potential. Even the De Beers marketing team knew it when they rejected Gerety's slogan, believing that it wouldn't resonate with audiences due to being grammatically incorrect.

And that, right there, highlights the main problem marketers have with the language of an audience: it can be incredibly elusive.

When the De Beers marketing team rejected Gerety's slogan, they did so truly believing that they knew better. They thought that they understood how their audience spoke and communicated. They thought that formal grammar was important to their audience. The eventual popularity of Gerety's slogan couldn't have proved them more wrong.

The same is true for countless other brands that misunderstood the language of their audience. GAP's rebranding mistake was meant to align with a young, hip audience but was instead compared to a budget airline. Dove's Real Beauty bottles were meant to align with the body-positive concepts they had been promoting for fifteen years but were instead met with shock and discomfort.

Joining the conversation that is already taking place is important. The key to doing that, however, is being able to identify what that conversation is and how it is taking place. The language of an audience does that by defining an audience and how they engage through the language they use.

Active Versus Passive Segments

As you work on building out audience segments, it's important to consider the differences between active and passive consumers. Active consumers are those already engaged with your product and brand. These consumers know what they want and have a clear idea of what your brand does to provide for that requirement. In some cases, these consumers are a stereotype of your industry, and the language of your industry probably already speaks to them—at least to some degree.

Then there are passive segments. These groups are filled with consumers who have an idea of what they want but aren't sure of the specifics. They are a goal-driven group, currently in discovery mode. They often make up the vast majority of consumers, but they're also much harder to target. To align your brand with this group, it's important to know what their goal is and align that with the existing language of your industry.

I mentioned a tech startup I had worked with. Over the course of a year, the brand had done an excellent job of increasing organic traffic to the site. But it hadn't increased sales. The content that was created appealed to the active segment of users—those who knew what they wanted. However, with the industry being so competitive, those users had already chosen the brand they wanted to support.

If we had instead used Shift to modify our content to match the passive audience, and appeal to their emotional needs rather than logical ones, we would have likely seen a sales increase that mirrored that traffic increase—especially within the timeframe of one year.

Passive segments aren't necessarily looking for your product. They are, however, still potential consumers—especially down the line. As a result, it's important that while you continue to target active consumers over time, you also bring awareness to passive consumers so that when they're ready to purchase, you're already there.

Defining Value for an Audience

When I began creating that second corpus for the tech startup, I immediately faced a problem. How could I properly define a single audience to the point that I would be able to draw high-level conclusions reliably? While search and machine language systems have come a long way in the last ten years, they are still far behind a human's ability to intuitively assign attributes to a piece of content.

Conducting a large-scale search of the keyword "travel", for instance, would provide me with a garbled mess of content. Yes, I would see content from my target audience (if I were a travel brand), but I would also see content from other brands. This content would *contaminate* the results. Afterall, I'm not interested in the language of brands, I'm interested in the language of an audience.

Unlike brands, consumers create and engage with content online with the purpose of answering an emotional need. Whether that's to drive gratification, a sense of purpose, or something else, their fundamental reason for engaging is different than that of brands. Brands, ultimately, engage to sell. If you're a marketer and you're not thinking about how your engagement strategy links back to revenue, you're not doing it right.

This means that when exploring the language of an audience, it's important to drive a distinction between the language of brands and the language of audience. The two are different. While they may express similar topics, brands aim to promote their business, consumers aim to engage. This subtlety often manifests itself in the language used.

At first, this seems to throw a spanner into the works. Modern brands are all but omnipresent across all channels. This makes creating large scale corpora based on audience language alone impossible. Instead, it would seem that small scale corpora with brand content manually removed is the best a marketer can do.

When Waldon and Gale began conducting their research, I'm sure that they too were aware of the gaps in their methodologies. Real life data, regardless of the source, is almost never clean—especially when found and compiled on a large scale. Waldon's data missed real insight into the thought processes of his audience, while Gale's required consumers to knowingly give feedback—which potentially contaminated it. Yet they persevered, and over time their methodologies adjusted and changed to provide a more complete and reliable picture.

When I conducted that second study of language for the tech startup, I created only one corpus. That corpus contained over 100,000 pieces of user-generated content. It was compiled from social posts, community forums, and support questionnaires. At the time, I knew that social posts and community forums would include the language of brands. Brands frequently use those channels as a part of their engagement strategy. However, as I started to pull through the data, what I found was something that I hadn't considered: *the idea that the language of brands isn't always just the language of brands. Sometimes, it becomes the language of an audience too.*

Social Networks are designed to encourage engagement. Books have been written, webinars performed, entire conferences created, all with the purpose of teaching marketers how to increase engagement on social media. Simon Sinek (remember him?) is often mentioned in social media engagement conversations, his concept of the "why statement" supporting many expert claims that engagement is resonation.

Consumers engage with content that they like: *with what they identify with*. They like and retweet and share and send to coworkers and friends and family. When a piece of content is shared by a user—regardless of whether it is because of its why statement or because of its creative, or anything else – it tells us that it speaks to an audience. In our case, our audience. Engagement signifiers, then, are key to the validity of large-scale corpora being able represent the language of an audience accurately. In other words, if content is engaged with and shared frequently, regardless of whether it was created by a consumer or by a brand, it is an example of the language of an audience.

When creating the second corpus for the tech startup, this meant that I needed a way to signify engagement. This was incredibly simple as most social APIs (the programming framework used to extract large scale collections of messages from them) represent engagement through duplication. In other words, if a message is shared three times, it will feature three times in the corpus. Needless to say, when conducting analysis, this meant that posts that engaged well would stand out.

Yet while the corpus definitely indicated language that *resonated* with the audience. It didn't necessarily represent *their* language. To make sure that it represented *their* language, another, secondary corpus, would be needed to triangulate the results. This is what I'll refer to as a **study B.**

Study B, like the first study, is also comprised of data pulled from channels that consumers engage with. However, instead of focusing on user-generated content specifically, it focuses on language that resonates with consumers. The difference is that instead of pulling content from product or service specific keywords and phrases, it is pulled from other brands that consumers also like, regardless of the industry.

To explain this, let's walk back into segments for a minute. Segments, when broken down enough, all meet some specific criteria. For Coca Cola, that may have included a segment of individuals who enjoy their beverages every day and another that liked them only occasionally. For Nike, it may mean a segment of athletes and a segment of sport amateurs. Each of these segments have things that band individual consumers together into a cohesive whole. One of the things you've defined, the others are opportunities for you to discover.

Modern analytics tools now allow us to take these segments and see what else they have in common, easily. What other brands do they like, what other content do they engage with, what websites do they frequent? As marketers, we now how access to an incredible amount of information with just a few clicks of a button. This is information we should be using to better understand our audience.

Study B takes the language used by brands and websites and content that your audience engage with, regardless of their association, and it turns it into a data set that can be used to confirm the findings of study A.

So in order to find the language of an audience, there are two studies you need to engage in:

Study A: What language does an audience use and engage with around a specific product or service.

Study B: What other brands resonate with an audience and what language do those brands use that is being engaged with?

While these studies use different corpus data, they both follow the same process of analysis: Locate high-frequency tokens and collocates, identify leading topics and themes, and identify emotional resonance. Since we've already covered how to locate high-frequency tokens and collocates and how to identify leading topics and themes previously, the only area left to cover is how to identify emotional resonance.

Finding Emotional Resonance

Brands that do well seek to challenge the conventions of their industry. They do this by finding opportunities. These opportunities are created by consumers and are embodied in their wants, needs, and desires. When we looked at the psychology of branding, I mentioned the power of emotion. This is what these opportunities present: clear methods for finding and driving emotional resonance.

The content I created for the tech startup didn't drive emotional resonance. Instead, it remained firmly rooted in the language of the industry. It offered solutions to logical needs, while entirely ignoring the emotional needs of consumers.

Conversely, Coca-Cola, with its Christmas Santa campaigns, provided solutions to emotional needs. Coca-Cola used Christmas to embody family spirit, happiness, and jolliness. Nike, with its "Just Do It" ads, answers the individual need to do well and succeed. De Beers answers the need for commitment and longevity of romance. Apple, with its innovative campaigns and designs, answers the need for innovation and freshness.

These brands all succeed because they align their existence with the emotional needs of their audience. Not multiple emotional needs, but a single, powerful emotional need that exists across all of their audience segments in some shape or form.

Finding emotional resonance means analyzing the language of your audience. Digging deep into their linguistic choices is key to providing insights into the emotions that drive their decision-making processes. To do this, you must return to study A and study B.

Firstly, looking at study B, you must ask yourself what those brands all have in common. Just like McDonald's did when they rebranded with the "I'm Lovin' It" campaign and realigned their messaging around the pop music industry. What is it about the other brands and industries that your audience engages with that is distinct?

If we look at web hosting, we find that consumers also like Blue Apron, National Geographic, Nordstrom, and Patrón Tequila. In terms of emotional triggers, this tells us that this group seeks to become capable of the financial posturing that sees them traveling the world, drinking fine beverages, and eating only the best food. These brands all directly align with the concept of entrepreneurship. As a result, this is their aspirational and emotional trigger.

Secondly, taking a look at study A, you must analyze the language your audience uses around your product or service already. It is important to state here that product or service is different from brand. We are not interested, necessarily, in what they say about our brand—you should already know that. What we are interested in, however, is how they talk about other brands or other products. What tokens and topics come up repeatedly in these conversations?

When consumers talk about your industry and your brand, they have a certain language for doing so—a certain set of semantics that may in part be defined by you and the other businesses in your industry, but are in large part from the audience themselves. This is different from the language of industry. While it still focuses on the industry, it does so from the perspective of the consumers, not brands. As a result, it is not the actual language of the industry, but the language of consumers who engage with the industry.

Knowing this is important for two reasons. One, consumers have their own perspectives on how the industry works. In some industries, brands will perpetuate ideas and conventions that do not resonate with audiences. Usually, a quick analysis here will find this disconnect. I have worked in several industries where this was the case.

The second reason this is important is because it helps to consolidate the language and trends you found with other brands. You should have access to a huge list of words and phrases that define your audience. However, not all of that language is going to resonate properly or fit within Shift. As we move into the final section of this book, having a clear idea of what that language should look like is key to making the right choices.

11

Driving Shift

Let's return, for a moment, to the psychology of branding I talked about earlier. The crux of brand recognition, if you remember, is the container. It is here where consumers place the concepts and conventions they associate with a brand. This can be the colors, the lexicon, a slogan, and more. All of these elements combine to create a language. Most consumers need to be exposed to this language five to seven times for that container to become easily retrievable, and even then, each marketing touchpoint they engage with can dismantle it.

The container, then, requires constant upkeep and iteration. Consumers require consistent exposure, with consistent resonance, in order for that container to be maintained and remain distinct. Even with this iteration in a constant state of flux, competitors will continue to push against your brand, creating their own standards for concepts and conventions. This is true no matter what your brand is. Even Apple, with its monolithic status in the tech industry, is required to iterate and change in relation to its competition.

At the beginning of this book, I provided a quote from the linguist Teun A. van Dijk: "Control over discourse and its properties are forms of the direct enactment of social or institutional power." This quote summarizes, almost perfectly, how brands are required to change and shift. Power, in the branding world, is being able to make your brand distinct and stand out from the competition. A brand that excels is a brand that dominates consumer interest and creates advocates seemingly effortlessly. Control over the discourse and conventions surrounding a brand, then, means being able to control distinction.

The tech startup, while creating a brand that could have defined the industry it sat within, failed to resonate with its audience. As a result, it failed to show distinction and so was unable to create a unique and powerful psychological container in the minds of consumers. Not dissimilarly, GAP went too far in the opposite direction. They drove a rebrand based almost completely on what they thought their audience wanted, and they failed to balance it with what their audience expected. As a result, the brand broke expectations and caused consumers to turn away in discomfort.

In another example, Dove's marketing team, with their Real Beauty bottles, were unable to see beyond the iterative success they had been implementing. Their marketing moved too far from the foundation that had been set by the industry; a foundation made up of the social and discourse conventions that their consumers had learned throughout their lives.

Unfortunately, in my experience, many brands tend to gravitate towards either focusing too heavily on audience language or industry language. They ignore the need for balance, and in doing so lose their ability to create distinction. Sometimes it's because their marketing teams don't properly understand their audience or their industry. Most of the time, it's because they believe that either reinventing the wheel or following the crowd will lead to success.

To provide experiences like Apple, or McDonald's, or Nike, or De Beers, it's important to not just follow conventions, but to drive them in new and unique directions, at a pace consumers can match. Within Shift, it is the industry and audience languages that enable brands to do this. Social and discourse conventions create and shape these languages. Understanding them gives you control over the discourse and, therefore, social and institutional conventions. In other words, by understanding the language of an audience and of an industry, you are able to define how an industry speaks to its consumers and how those consumers make purchases.

McDonald's has done this. Apple has done this. Nike, too. Now, it is your brand's turn to do this, by driving Shift.

The Need for Hope

For brands to remain top-of-mind, their touchpoints must remain consistent. Many brands do this by maintaining a brand voice and style throughout all of their marketing assets. Some brands extend this to a particular lexicon for fueling discourse: the use of similar tokens and phrases. As we looked at previously, Apple almost certainly has a particular lexicon for talking about its products; a lexicon directly linked to its brand promise of innovation.

Regardless of whether a brand has a formal lexicon, it's clear that successful brands make sure their marketing content falls within specific semantic fields. McDonald's, for instance, would never use the language of De Beers, who would never use the language of Nike. These brands have specific identities that they have crafted and iterated upon for decades. And we recognize them.

Think of your favorite brand. It can be anything you like, but it needs to be a brand. Think of the elements that brand maintains and that remain consistent throughout each of its touchpoints. For example, with Apple it may be the minimalist design. With McDonald's, it may be the happy color scheme and imagery. With Nike, it may be the high-pressure, competitive nature of its advertising campaigns. Now that you've thought of something, go to that brand's website and see how much the content there lines up with what you remember. If you're dealing with a brand that has maintained consistent marketing, it should be pretty similar.

But what happens when a brand needs to change? When McDonald's rebranded around the "I'm Lovin' It" campaign, they took their brand in a different direction. While they maintained the general style guidelines they had previously, they reworked them to put forward a newer, more youthful image. Coca-Cola, similarly, has moved on from the print advertisements of the 1940s and now projects a youthful, modern appearance. While the jolly Santa still features in some of their advertisements, they have also added polar bears to their Christmas campaigns.

These changes, as we have covered, are vital to the survival of a brand. Iteration is as core to brand identity as its style and voice guidelines are. So how does a brand maintain consistency in the face of continued, iterative change?

To understand how, we must take another look at Escalas and Bettman's research. Escalas and Bettman, as you will recall, studied why consumers decide to purchase from one brand over another. They found that core to purchasing intent was identity. As they state: "consumers use brands whose images match reference groups to which they belong, [and they] establish a psychological association with those groups." In other words, the ability for a consumer to identify with one brand over another is what causes them to purchase from that brand.

For example, when consumers purchase from Coca-Cola instead of Pepsi, they do so because they identify with the brand of Coca-Cola more. Think back to the two slogans used by Coca-Cola and Pepsi in the early 2000s:

Life Tastes Good

Dare for More

When I introduced these slogans originally, I did so without telling you where they came from. I asked you to choose the one you preferred, and I then explained why, psychologically, you made that choice. In simple terms, the first slogan is relaxing; the second is competitive. If you are more of a relaxed person, then you likely chose the first. If you are more of an adventurous person, you probably chose the second.

This is self-identification. It's the ability for you to take content and touchpoints shared by a brand and say to yourself "that's something I agree with" or "that's not something I agree with." The ability for brands to identify with consumers is key to securing resonance. And resonance is key to building recognition. However, for resonance to be truly powerful, the message needs to emotionally resonate. As Antonio Damasio proved, making decisions and evaluating brands requires emotions.

The brands we have looked at in this book have all been from different industries. They have all sold different products to different audiences, with different strategies and different brand guidelines. They have all created unique identities that different consumer groups associate and identify with. But they have all maintained consistency across these touchpoints in the same way: by creating a single, overarching narrative that builds on aspiration and hope.

Apple's message of innovation speaks to the hope for a bold new future. McDonald's "I'm Lovin' It" messaging speaks to the hope of vitality and youth. De Beers' "A Diamond Is Forever" speaks to the hope of commitment and a long-lasting marriage. Nike speaks to the hope of success. Even Umbricius Scaurus, with his pungent fish sauce and "the flower of" slogan, speaks to the hope of a fish sauce that doesn't smell bad. Every brand covered in this book, every brand that resonates memorably and carves its unique niche, does so by ultimately revolving its message around the concept of hope.

This isn't to say the other emotions do not have their own place. However, think back to Jonah Berger's research. He found that across 7,000 different news articles published by the New York Times, positive articles were shared much more than negative ones. This was true even when negative content was more surprising, interesting, or practically useful. The same is true for brands. It's positive brands and content that consumers want to share with friends, family, and coworkers. And brands that are shared more grow bigger.

For years, the sports apparel industry did little more than push logical solutions with a side of American sport fanaticism. Few other businesses looked to revolutionize the industry or market their shoes as keys to success. After all, they were just shoes—it is the individual who carves out success, not footwear. Right?

For Nike, the disconnect came with what audiences expected from the footwear industry and what they really wanted. The same is true of other brands as well. Fast-food chains were not speaking to the rhetoric of youth; they instead focused on speed—a feature of their product, not a result of its use. For Apple, competitors had long talked about the technical specifications of their products, assuming audiences would assess them in respect to logical factors. It was Apple who first appealed to their audience's desire for something new and innovative, thereby emotionally resonating through aspiration and hope.

For brands to become distinct, they need to push their audience in a new direction: one that causes the brand container to—while remaining simple—become distinct. The emotions of hope and aspiration are critical to this process. They fuel action and create marketing journeys. Brands like McDonald's, Apple, and Coca-Cola offer consumers the opportunity to complete this journey by satisfying their emotional desires. In other words, they offer consumers the ability to fulfil their aspirations by delivering on what the brand positions as hope.

Linking this back to the psychological container, these aspirations drive the emotional resonance required for the container (and so the brand) to become and remain distinct. They drive the ability for consumers to identify with a brand consistently, across all touchpoints, even when content is dissimilar or a major rebrand occurs. It is these aspirations that bring together a brand under a single, overarching narrative and story. And it is these aspirations that are the driving force of Shift.

Balancing Hope with Expectation

Brands can't stray too far from their industry's rhetoric. When they do so too quickly, they alienate themselves from their audience. Remember, uncertainty registers in the brain much like an error does and creates a feeling of discomfort. Too many inconsistencies push against an individual's "container". This, in turn, leads to them feeling enough discomfort so as to ignore, or even object to, a brand.

However, when small, minor adjustments are made, complemented by elements that reinforce existing expectations, they can be channeled to create memorable experiences that reinforce a unique "brand container". Linguistically, finding this equilibrium is a case of balancing the social and discourse conventions of an audience with the semantic fields of an industry. This is the essence of Shift.

When McDonald's realigned their marketing message with the "I'm Lovin' It" campaign, they engaged in Shift. They found what their audience wanted—youth and vitality—and they shifted their industry's rhetoric—the idea of the American burger—to better align with that. They didn't do it overnight. Rather, they engaged in a long and drawn-out campaign. De Beers did the same with the diamond industry by realigning their industry's rhetoric around the notion of marriage and commitment and pulling away from the long, complicated prose of the past. Nike did the same with sportswear.

The full framework for Shift accounts for these changes. It centers around the idea of the Shift container—a psychological container that contains consumer ideas of the brand. To the left lies the rhetoric of your industry—the semantic and lexical fields associated with businesses like yours. To the right lies the hopes of your audience—the social and discourse conventions that align with the type of content they digest.

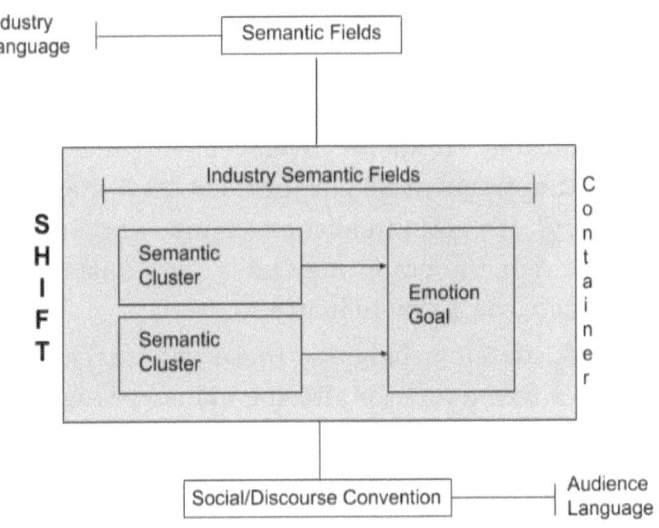

Aligning convention and semantics drives shift.

When I decided on the direction we would take with the tech startup, I focused too heavily on industry language. The lexicon, style, and tone were all influenced by other brands in the industry, all of whom were competing with logical solutions to logical problems. While this choice resonated well with the machine algorithm of search engines, it failed to resonate with the organic emotions of consumers.

Focusing too much on the competition and aligning your brand with the brands that surround it is a bad direction. In part, this can be explained by the nature of the psychological container of a brand. By duplicating everything that already exists within an industry, it's impossible to be distinct.

The same would have happened had the brand instead focused solely on audience language. By flouting what is expected of brands in its industry, it would have been unrecognizable. Audience engagement and lexicon showed that frequent tokens included "new", "explore", and "story". It's not unrealistic to think, with language like this, that the brand may have been mistaken for belonging to the travel industry.

The Shift container balances these two extremes and provides a framework for altering industry language to better match that of audience language. Just like when shifting gears in a car, this is an iterative process that relies on modular changes.

So Shift is a thing. But it's also a complicated thing. The individual aspects of brand voice, persona identification, and SEO are important, but they simply don't work in isolation or when not part of a wider, more focused strategy. But of course, this book isn't about typical marketing or strategy; it's about language. As I mentioned earlier, powerful brands do more than just evoke concepts; they evoke aspirational concepts, and they do so in a way that shifts and reinforces consumers' concepts of self. It's the language of brands that does this.

The Language of Brands

To find language that will fit inside the Shift container, a good first step is to search industry language and audience language and identify overlap. What tokens, concepts, and topics exist in both? In many cases, this will provide a small foundation, but not an entire lexicon. To create the lexicon, you will have to go further.

Defining the language of Shift is as much about combining the language of industry and the language of audience as it is about creating the language yourself. The language of Shift doesn't have to be restricted to just the language that consumers already encounter; it may be that you can pull in language from somewhere else.

At the same time, the language has to resonate with the brand guidelines you've discovered and set. Certain industries do speak in certain ways, and changing this pattern can do more harm than good. Technology businesses, for instance, tend to avoid adjectives. Replacing that lexicon with one that contains an abundance of them is going to startle the audience and destroy any chance of resonating. When identifying the language of an industry, you should have created a tone and style guide. The purpose of this guide is to help you create language for Shift. It provides a concrete framework for doing so.

At the same time, it's important to consider the concept of hope specific to your audience, as identified in the audience language study. With the tech startup, the concept of adventure functioned as a resonating idea. This means identifying language that builds on adventure while also maintaining status as a part of the tech industry. "New", "Build", and "Explore" would all work very well; "escapade", "caper", and "feat" would not.

Therefore, there are two factors you must consider when creating a lexicon.

- It cannot radically depart from audience expectations
- It must create an opportunity to inspire audience-specific hope

Consolidating language into a usable format means picking out only the language that is the most important and dropping the majority of the lexicon you have discovered.

This new lexicon, while linked to the holistic approach of the brand, should be separated into individual segments. Each of these segments should target a specific audience of your brand. These are what we will call semantic clusters—in other words, meaning clusters.

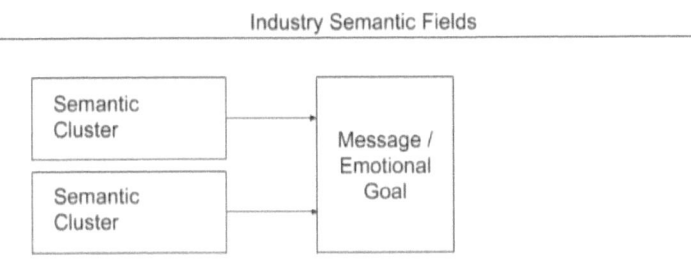

The reason for segmented semantic clusters should be obvious. One brand often has multiple audiences. Each audience needs to be spoken to on its own terms. Each semantic cluster contains this language. However, they are also required to adhere to the industry semantic fields found previously, and all semantic clusters should direct consumers to the same message and emotional goal. This is required for brand coherence. This is laid out in the diagram.

Here, the limitations of the industry are highlighted above. This is the framework within which a brand can exist without causing consumer discomfort. These guidelines can be defined by looking at the language of the industry.

Take, for instance, the language associated with Apple's audience and innovation. This language follows the basic principles of the tech industry. It's simple and easy to follow. There are some adjectives, but they're infrequent and basic. At the same time, the language conforms to existing expectations outlined by the industry. It doesn't actually "innovate" all that much— certainly not as much as its audience believes. Instead, it builds on the base that has been set by others and creates something that is different enough to stand out and remain memorable, while similar enough to conform to expectations.

But in order for Shift to work, it requires iteration. That means that it needs to keep changing.

Engaging in Turn-Taking

A car does not make its way from 0 to 60 in a single gear. Rather, it shifts, making its way through the different gears as it ramps up its output and power. Lower gears allow for less power to be consumed while initiating the processes required for speed. Higher gears build on the momentum of the lower gears to generate that speed. It is these shifts that provide a car with the ability to make headway in the beginning and deliver results later on. All gears have their place, and losing any one of them would mean radical changes to the functional ability of a car.

Similarly, Shift is not completed in a single marketing move. As I have outlined throughout this book, Shift is both an idea and a practice. In order for it to be successful, it needs to be integrated into your marketing efforts throughout, and continually implemented and iterated on. It is not one single, encapsulating move, but a series of smaller changes aimed at building momentum and generating results. It is for this reason that turn-taking is a vital component in any Shift strategy.

I discussed turn-taking previously and used Coca-Cola's Christmas advertisements as an example of how turn-taking works. If they had initially delivered the image of Santa Claus we now know and love today, then it would likely have never become the iconic image it has. Instead, they iterated on changes, eventually releasing a version of Santa that was the product of over a decade of turn-taking. Often, this iteration leads to brands that continue to resonate well with audiences.

As a brand develops in relation to Shift, so too does its audience and its industry. An important part of Shift is making sure to track and monitor these changes so that your response—as a brand—shows an awareness of these changes. Monitoring these changes is simply a case of committing to iterative studies into the language of audience and industry. You create something, your audience responds, you listen.

This isn't only important in relation to your brand. Other competitors in the industry will adapt to the changes you begin to create. Think back to when I mentioned this quote from Henry Ford:

> *If I had asked people what they*
> *wanted, they would have said faster*
> *horses.*

I used it previously to describe how consumers don't know what they want—that it's the marketer's responsibility to find out what that is. However, as should have become clear while reading this book, knowing what is happening in your industry is vital to success. It's not the full picture, but it's still an important part of the picture. What many marketers don't think about in relation to that quote is that, yes, initially, consumers did not know that they wanted a car. However, after Ford released the first Model T, consumers did know. Other brands in the same industry listened to those consumers, and in doing so they were able to eat away at Ford's market share.

As your brand begins to increasingly align its marketing with the language of audience and sees success, other brands in your industry will react. They will, in most cases, seek to duplicate that success, changing it slightly to match their own brand image. This creates a continually evolving ecosystem that is predominantly reactionary.

However, there is a difference between brands that use Shift and those that react. While others are looking to compete in areas that already exist, Shift brands are constantly looking forward and for something new. In terms of turn-taking, others seek to dwell on the same conversation points and topics time and time again, while Shift brands are always listening for the next one.

12

Measuring Shift

To bring about Shift in your company, you'll need to gain buy-in from your organization's leadership. This means being able to measure and show value as Shift drives revenue and growth.

However, while Shift does drive results, like most marketing strategies, it is a process. Similar to modern SEO strategies, big results don't happen overnight. Implementing Shift requires a commitment to long-term growth and change. Yet while this doesn't necessarily mean an immediate increase in sales, there are metrics you can measure to chart the progression of Shift and show success to stakeholders. It's important that you set expectations before engaging with Shift.

As with all marketing strategies, what you measure really depends on what your goal is. If you're looking for brand awareness, then awareness metrics should be central to campaign reporting. If you're looking for revenue growth, then conversion statistics should be at the center of those reports.

That being said, Shift's progressive nature lends itself to a specific blueprint for reporting and growth, covering three key areas: engagement, awareness, and growth.

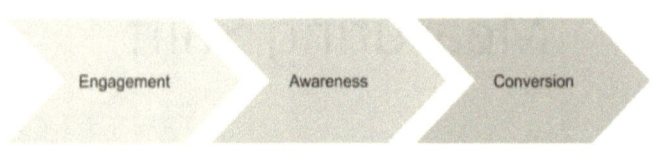

Stage 1: Engagement

As you initially roll out Shift, you should begin to notice an increase in engagement. Your first Shift should almost immediately provide data on whether the direction you've identified resonates with your audience. If it resonates particularly well, then the content you're creating and sharing should start to see higher engagement.

Social posts should see an increase in likes and shares. Web pages should see higher click-through rates, as should paid advertisements and any meta description or title changes you make. As you continue to build out and iterate, you should begin to see this engagement continue to grow, with new types of consumers joining your existing base. Brand mentions across social platforms will increase, and recommendations at events and conferences will start to become a mainstay. You'll also likely begin to see an increase in user-generated content in the form of reviews.

It's here where you start to build brand advocates. Brand advocates are those who believe in your brand so much that they will happily share it with others and promote its value. Once you begin to build up brand advocates, you will know that your brand is resonating, and your Shift implementation is heading in the right direction.

Remember, engagement is a vital stage for building and driving your brand strategy. It is here where careful measurement of change success will help you to see if those changes are resonant or if you need to return to the drawing board.

Stage 2: Awareness

As you begin to draw in an increasing number of brand advocates, you can expect to see an increase in brand awareness. The user-generated content the brand advocates create will reach an increasing number of consumers, without you having to pay a single buck.

Awareness can be measured by looking at site traffic and analyzing share of voice across social platforms. These metrics should show a steady increase as awareness and engagement increase. Over time, those who are introduced to your brand will become further advocates, leading to even more awareness.

When awareness begins to plateau, this indicates that it's time to perform the next iteration of Shift. This will gradually help you to increase your influence over consumers and your industry.

Stage 3: Conversion

As advocates and engagement grow, so too will conversions start to increase. This will begin much more slowly at first. Advocates, in many cases, will only buy one or two of your products or services, and it will take time for their promotions to circulate. However, once sales start to increase, you should see a steady increase continue (while also accounting for any sales trends you've seen in the past).

Initially, it's worthwhile measuring the impact of your content and Shift by looking at the different ways in which conversions are occurring. If you're finding an increase in direct purchases over sales calls, then chances are your Shift is resonating incredibly well. Consumers are "trusting their gut" and making purchases based on the emotional resonance you've created.

Alternatively, if you're seeing more sales calls and few direct purchases, but consumers are purchasing larger quantities or service levels, then your Shift is also performing well. This is especially true in B2B industries, where networking is core to successful partnerships.

Remember, consistently measuring and reporting on these metrics is key to identifying and securing success. The results you find here won't only help you to secure organizational buy-in but will also inform successive iterations of Shift. Once you begin seeing improvement, you can continue to build on it well into the future.

13

Conclusion

Shift it not a magic bullet. As much as I wish I could say that results will happen overnight, they won't. This is true of any worthwhile marketing solution that helps to build a brand for long-term success.

However, once you've invested in Shift and started to see the needle move, results tend to increase exponentially. As consumers begin to relate more with your brand, they will begin to share it with friends, family and colleagues. Shift is designed to enable and attract these advocates, helping your business to grow organically instead of through expensive advertisements with low conversion rates. Shift also gives you back control of your business.

Often, when brands and businesses don't know how to proceed, they hire consultants or bring in agencies to help. These agencies then compile reports based on disjointed accounts and decontextualized data. Often, these reports only show a small piece of the picture and serve to reinforce the industry-standard rhetoric already in place. The problem with this is that the existing rhetoric doesn't help a brand to become distinct. In fact, it does exactly the opposite: It makes brands mediocre.

I learned this when employing an earlier version of Shift. While the brand resonated very well with the language of the industry and found itself ranking for crucial keywords on search engines, it lacked the emotional oomph to convert those organic views into conversions. And when I instead focused solely on the language of audience in an earlier project, I found that it both did not rank well organically, nor did it emotionally resonate enough to raise conversions. As explored throughout this book, this is likely due to the disconnect that audiences found between the content and experiences they expected and the content that they wanted.

Both sides of the coin need to be kept in mind when creating new content. This helps brands to follow the four core functions of brand:

- To communicate
- To relate
- To resonate
- To inspire

By following these four pillars, you'll be able to direct consumers to experiences they want.

You've come to this book looking for a new strategy, one which works where others have failed. This strategy means venturing into territories you likely haven't in the past. It means learning and adopting methodologies that most of your competitors aren't even aware of. It means *Shift*.

For over a decade I've worked on creating Shift; an idea born from the world of linguistic academia. Shift has grown to encapsulate more than just understanding the language of brands. It has become a methodology for being able to create a language for your brand that is both distinct and memorable.

It does this based on an understanding of how we, as individuals, interact and engage with language. When we compare the advertisements of the 1960s with those of today, we see clear disconnects with the type of content. They use different wording, distinct visuals, unique designs, and are based on different social and discourse conventions. These elements all comprise the *language* of that content. Instead of looking at them individually, it's important that marketers begin looking at them holistically.

You can do this by identifying the language of your audience and the language of your industry. Both offer valuable insights into wants and expectations respectively. Once you've identified these two areas, you're then able to create a clear framework for brand progression and iteration.

And that is the key to Shift: *iteration*. Brands evolve and change. Not necessarily the products themselves—Coca Cola, for example, has used the same formula since its inception (minus a mistake in the 80s). However, as consumers digest more content and businesses find new opportunities, the conventions that surround them adapt to new information.

In fact, the very concept of marketing has changed as digital channels have become more mainstream and consumers have gained access to increasingly large and varied amounts of content. Take delivery mechanisms as an example: TV increased in popularity, with everyone having a television set in their home. Then attention moved to the internet, where individuals would consume information through banner ads and web searches. Now, mobile takes a dominant position, with consumers able to acquire and digest information wherever they are at the touch of a button.

Shift recognizes that change occurs and thereby places three key points of iteration for every project:

- Understanding convention
- Realizing position
- Inspiring distinction

As you begin to adopt a continual process of Shift, you'll notice changes to awareness, engagement, and conversions. You'll also see a change in the number of consumers becoming advocates of your brand. Brand advocacy is key to Shift and acts as one of the pillars it is built on. This is because brand advocacy is one of the fundamental necessities for prolonged, organic growth.

Throughout this book we explored the language of brands. We looked beyond just high-level similarities to identify core foundations for consumer thought and desire. We looked at the way in which industries define their constituents and how "revolutionary" content cannot always be as revolutionary as you want it to be; and, in fact, often isn't as revolutionary as everyone thinks it is. But most of all, we've identified at a method for applying knowledge to practice, to make a brand distinct.

Now it is your turn to take your brand and turn it into something amazing and distinct. By all of us doing this, we'll create a world where businesses create organic, meaningful and resonant content and experiences, and we'll never have to deal with a piece of spam again.

Acknowledgements

For almost a decade, I have worked to develop a better understanding of the language we use as individuals, businesses, and brands. *Shift,* as it is today, is a version of that understanding. It is something that has been molded by countless influences and many individuals— too many to list here. However, to finish this book without acknowledging the people who have helped to make this a reality would be a disservice to them.

I'll begin by mentioning those who supported me as I wrote and crafted the ideas in this book. Firstly, those around me: my family and friends, who provided feedback and support. I will forever be indebted for the time you spent reading over what I can only imagine being arduous first drafts and hearing me ramble about ideas that hadn't been finished. Also, to those who I worked with over the last decade: thank you for hearing me out and being a part of Shift.

I would also like to say thank you to the brands and businesses that trusted me when I presented them with the ideas I've outlined in this book. I especially want to thank those who kept faith even when results weren't immediate. As I was taught early on in my career, success is iteration: *never stop moving forward.*

I would like to mention the work of countless linguists who have worked on and set the foundation for the linguistic theory that has been mentioned in this book. Vitally, the work of those in the field of Critical Discourse Analysis, including Teun A. van Dijk, Ruth

Wodak, Theo Van Leeuwen, and Christopher Hart. I would also like to thank those who have contributed to the area of corpus linguistics – and taught me when I was a student – vitally including Paul Baker and Geoffrey Leech. And a list of acknowledgements wouldn't be complete without mentioning other linguists and semioticians I have been lucky enough to meet and learn from over the last decade, including Daniel Chandler, Elena Semino, Willem Hollmann, and many more.

Outside of linguistics, this book wouldn't have been possible without insights from notable academics in varying fields; including Daniel Kahnemen in the field of psychology and Neuroscientists Antonio Damasio, David Rock and Al Ringleb. I would also like to say thank you to the countless other studies and research conducted by those committed to building a better understanding of how the mind works.

Upon writing this book, I also leaned heavily on insights from other works, including *Black Swan* by Nassim Nicholas Taleb, *Start With Why* by Simon Sinek, *Storynomics* by Robert McKee and Thomas Gerace, *Nudge* by Cass Sunstein and Richard Thaler, and *Blink* by Malcom Gladwell.

Finally, to those who read this book and learn something. Especially, to those who read this book and use the ideas in it. Thank you. Thank you for giving it a shot and working to develop your brand into something more. Together, we can change the world.

Notes

Diagrams

Brand Pyramid

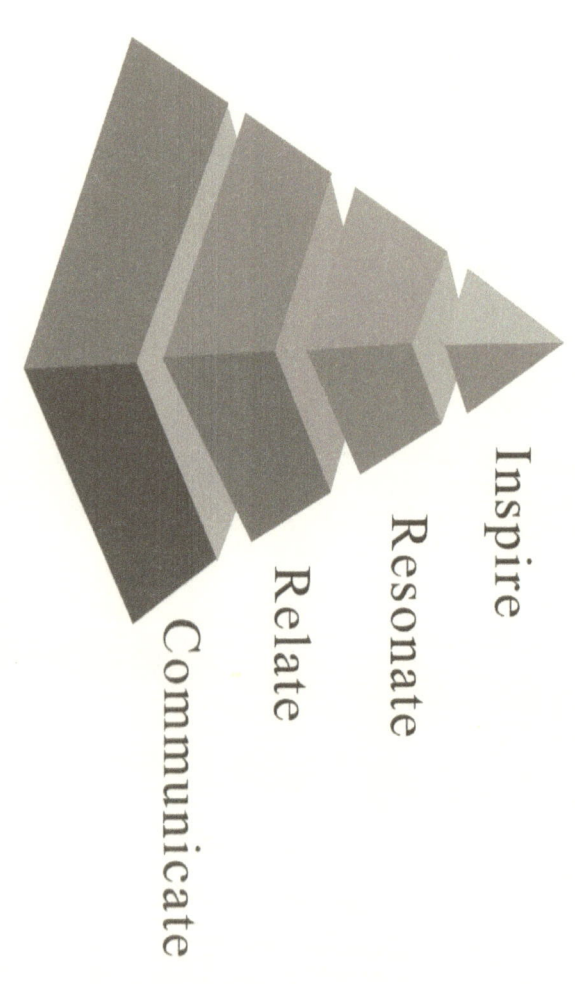

Shift

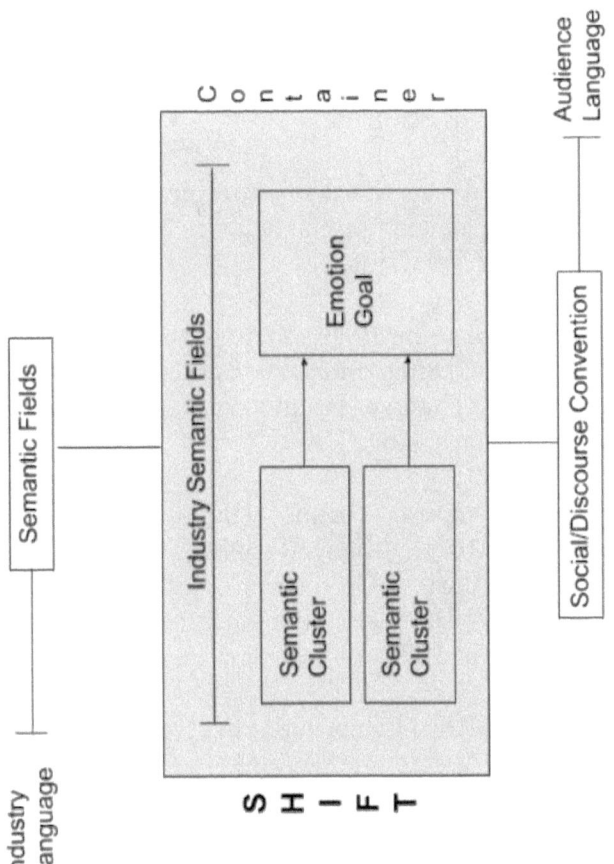

Part 1: A History of Branding

Why Language?

[1] Umbricius Scaurus' mosaic is often cited as being one of the first examples of marketing done right. He was very well known for his fish products, the most popular of which was called Garum. In most cases, he would brand the bottles the fish sauce came in with the slogan "from the shop of Scaurus."

Interestingly, it was thanks to samples of Garum from his home that modern archaeologists were able to date the eruption of Vesuvius.

[2] The longest running slogan in modern history actually belongs to the coffee manufacturer Maxwell House. Their "Good To The Last Drop" slogan has been running for over 100 years, since 1907.

[3] Antoine Bechara, Hanna Damasio, Antonio R. Damasio. (2000) Emotion, Decision Making and the Orbitofrontal Cortex. Cerebral Cortex. The Gambling task used by Damasio was originally created by Bechara et al. in 1994.

[4] Albert Costa, Alice Foucart, Sayuri Hayakawa, Melina Aparici, Jose Apesteguia, Joy Heafner, Boaz Keysar. Your Morals Depend on Language.

An important criticism of this study is that language wasn't the only factor in play. As outlined by writers such as Malcom Gladwell, it's very possible that more is going on. Dyslexic readers are more often more capable of processing complex information when given enough time. It's arguable that the increased processing requirements when thinking in a second language were the reason behind why the individuals were more likely to make rational decisions in their second language. In these instances, logic was able to overcome emotion.

[5] If you're interested in watching a handful of these ads, a lot of them are available on YouTube, including the famous "eel" sketch. While HSBC got better at portraying cultural differences over time, their original ads did not age well as the world became more globalized.

The Coca Cola Shift

[1] Haddon Sundblom took inspiration for his Santa Claus from the 1822 poem "A Night Before Christmas". It was this poem and its description of Santa that led Sundblom to conceive of him as a warm, happy and friendly character. While now known as "the guy who did Coca Cola Santa" he actually played a very significant role in 20th century advertising, both influencing other artists, and defining what the American Dream looked like with his pictures. Santa was just a part of that.

[2] The history of Santa Claus' portrayal is actually a very complicated one. Coca Cola, despite helping to mold the modern day image of Santa, was not the first to depict him as a jolly, happy character. Thomas Nast, whose artwork was said to have inspired Coca Cola's advertisements of the 20s, actually drew a rather Jolly Santa in 1881 for the poem A visit From St. Nicholas. His outfit, however, was different. This is perhaps

where the idea that Coca Cola made Santa red comes from.

[3] Saturday Evening Post cover by Norman Rockwell. 1920.

[4] The hypodermic needle model of advertising stated that audiences would accept and consume anything that was given to them. It assumed that audiences were incapable of individual thought or the ability to pick and mix the messages they wanted to engage with. Needless to say, this theory didn't last that long and advertisers who continued to advocate for it quickly went out of business.

[5] A fictional retelling of the McDonald's story can be seen in the film "The Founder".

[6] While De Beers is a great example of how powerful language can be when it's used correctly, the example used here is a slogan. Slogans are not the only powerful unit of language for use in marketing. As we look at throughout this book, they are just a small piece of a larger puzzle.

[7] This study was published in the Journal of behavioral decision making and used participants who did not have a history of engaging in gambling behavior. As a result, the decisions made here are not necessarily representative of addicted gamblers—but they are representative of the average person.

Part 2: How We Perceive Brand

How Does Language Work

[1] The question "Can pictures assert?" actually comes from the 20th century art historian Ernst Gombrich, who stated that "pictures cannot assert". In his view, statements cannot be translated into images. Meaning images cannot create their own units of meaning but rely on outside knowledge. Following this logic, written language also cannot assert.

[2] Panos Athanasopoulos et al. Two Languages, Two Minds: Flexible Cognitive Processing Driven by Language of Operation.

In the study, German speakers matched ambiguous scenes with goal-oriented scenes about 40% of the time, compared with 25% among English speakers. The conclusion drawn was that language played a role in shaping perception. Different languages mean different perceptions.

[3] Semiotics is considered a branch of philosophy, with philosophers throughout time exploring the relationship between signs and symbols. 20th century Semiotician Umberto Eco goes so far as to say that semiotics is implicit in the work of almost all major thinkers throughout history.

[4] If you want a good example of dialect in action, take a look at China. Some studies place the number of dialects in active use at more than 200. Some of these dialects are only used in very small geographic areas and by isolated communities. Simple words like I (我) are pronounced very differently by these different groups. In Mandarin it is pronounced "wo", in Cantonese it is pronounced "ngo", and in Wu it is

pronounce "ngu". Same meaning, same written form—different pronunciation.

[5] According to semioticians—academics who study the nature of signs and symbols—there is no actual connection between the signifier and the signified; they are, for all intents and purposes, arbitrary. For many semioticians, this describes language perfectly: S collection of signs and symbols given meaning for no particular reason other than convention.

[6] Eco's quote here highlights the nature of language and meaning. In one sense, as the world changes, language remains our only connection to the past. The rose of old may no longer exist, but its name remains. From another perspective, however, it talks to how we construct meaning. A "rose" as a sign refers only to the archetypal idea of a rose—it does not refer to a specific rose. In other words, when you read the word "rose", you think of what a rose is or could be—not an actual, real-life rose. After all, all roses are, in their own way, unique. All we possess then, as readers, are names (signs) and not actually roses (the signified).

The Origin of Meaning

[1] This comes from the work of Teun a. Van Dijk, a Dutch linguist famed for writing some of the core academic theory surrounding Critical Discourse Analysis (CDA). CDA views language as a social practice and focuses on how power relations are reinforced (or subverted) by texts.

[2] *The Old Man and the Bay* is just one of many media interpretations of Walt Stack. Countless other

publications have created their own. The LA Times wrote several pieces on him, and several other brands used him in ad campaigns, including Realtime Watch. In the film Forest Gump, Forest's endless running is heavily based on the life of Walt Stack and his insistence on completing a 17-mile run every day.

Creating a Story

[1] The story of the "A Diamond Is Forever" slogan is a fascinating one, with several different perspectives on how the line was originally perceived. Some sources claim that Gerety herself was unhappy with the line, while others say that it was the executive team. Regardless, the slogan would go to press a year after it was originally created and is still used in advertising campaigns by De Beers to this day.

[2] Storynomics has become one of the more interesting marketing works in recent years. Presenting marketing campaigns as stories, it walks marketers through how to create the types of stories that inspire a customer to action, instead of satisfaction. A lot of my own marketing practices outside of language have come from this book.

[3] The modern concept of the social actor in linguistics can be attributed to Van Leeuwen, who looked at how individuals and groups were represented in texts from both a grammatical and semantic perspective, and what that meant for social actors and their representation.

The Feature Fallacy

[1] Resonance is one of the most important aspects of great marketing. It combines both what you say and how you say it. Great copywriters know this and will often drop the catchy one liners for clear, simple exposition. If you're looking to bring on board a copywriter, a good test is to have them write one liners for a product and see if they focus on catchy or clear language. The latter will almost always perform better.

[2] We often see this take place in real life football advertisements, where the protagonist is either from a team that isn't polarizing or is obscured enough that they could be on any team. I recommend looking at Nike's "Change history with one strike" advertisements to see a clear example.

[3] Based on 2018 data from Counterpoint Research. By 2018, almost 100% of smartphones valued at over $800 included more than one camera, with only a few name brands holding out against the trend – including Samsung and Google.

[4] The HTC and LG offerings both saw a lack of marketing before being released. Instead, they relied on word of mouth. However, once released, some advertisements were pushed out, with RadioShack running an ad campaign for the HTC Evo 3D that included reference to the phone's dual camera capabilities.

[3] The release of the P9 was relatively close to that of the iPhone 7, so it's possible to argue that Huawei's device was the originator of dual camera popularity. However, this ignores the marketing effort

[6] The Megapixel war is a perfect example of marketing features vs benefits. When digital cameras first came

out, few people really understood how they worked and how to obtain better image quality. Megapixels actually had little impact on image quality, and instead the camera's sensor size was the defining factor.

Yet in an effort to provide an easy method for comparison, brands started to push the notion of more megapixels as meaning better image quality. Consumers latched on and saw more megapixels as being better. This wasn't because of anything to do with actual feature quality – after all, it wasn't megapixels that made a better-quality image. Instead, it was about having something that was better. The benefit went beyond the feature.

[7] The brand pyramid is an important consideration for both copywriters and designers. While the work of copywriters is often easier to judge and more visible, a designer's ability to translate copy into an easily digestible format requires a clear understanding of how the brand pyramid works in relation to the whole.

Part 3: Driving Shift

Picking Apart Language

[1] Microsoft's 2015 study should be taken with a grain of salt. The sample size is not entirely representative, and their results indicate that attention spans are decreasing by an unbelievable 88% every year. This would mean that at the time of writing this, in 2019, attention spans are just over 0.0128 seconds. Needless to say, that number doesn't add up.

[2] Kastner and her team's findings actually came when trying to study how individuals can pick out objects from cluttered environments—just like when consumers are presented with a page that includes a lot of information. They used a great metaphor to explain how human attention works, comparing it to a stage production. They state that while the spotlight it on most of the time, four times per second the house lights come on and attention is no longer on one thing.

[3] Dove's Real Beauty campaign has actually been one of the most successful marketing campaigns in history. The original campaign has become a staple in classes that focus on viral marketing and campaign techniques. Even today, Real Beauty campaigns are still run, building on their success from 2004.

[4] Corpus analysis is the analysis of large collections of texts to identify themes and styles. It can now be performed through computation methods. In essence, the internet is a large corpus and Google's ranking algorithm is a tool for analyzing and showing only relevant results. To conduct the analysis outlined in this book, you will need a corpus tool. I recommend AntConc as a free one for getting started.

[5] This phrase was first mentioned in The Boston Journal in 1885, with the writer stating that it was a good practice sentence for writing students.

[6] While a powerful tool for linguistics and marketers, frequency is also guilty of guiding many analysts to incorrect conclusions. On its own, it serves only to provide a high-level analysis of content and language choices. In order for it to truly provide value, frequency has to be used in conjunction with concordance line analysis.

[7] The actual wording used by Christoff et al. here was "mind wandering may be part of a larger class of mental phenomena that enable executive processes to occur without diminishing the potential contribution of the default network for creative thought and mental simulation. Although it may undermine our immediate goals, mind wandering may enable the parallel operation of diverse brain areas in the service of distal goals that extend beyond the current task."

[8] This may surprise you. However, since adjectives have been removed from the rhetoric in some industries, this leaves nouns and verbs as the most powerful units in copy. However, as with everything in marketing, there is always an exception.

[9] I first learned about Chomsky's Universal Grammar in university. In modern academia, you could even say that the very idea of such a fundamental is crazy. However, if you take a step back and look at some of Chomsky's foundational work here, you'll start to see that there was reasoning behind an idea that has now become more pop-culture than academia.

Language and Brand

[1] I'm British, so the Oxford English dictionary is my definition staple. However, taking a look at popular US dictionaries like Merriam-Webster shows similar definitions, including "a public image, reputation, or identity conceived of as something to be marketed or promoted".

[2] Patrick Davis has worked with fortune 100 companies for almost 2 decades. If there's anyone that knows about

the power of brand and how it can be used to distinguish a business, it's him.

[3] One of my favorite quotes about a brand being more significant than product comes from Marc Gobe, a marketer and author of the book Emotional Branding, and concerns Apple. He goes as far as to say that "the brand is all they've got," and "without the brand, Apple would be dead."

[4] This occurred when documentaries like Super Size Me exposed the fast food industry in pop-culture. The industry took a nosedive, with many of the big chains (like McDonald's) scrambling to realign their marketing efforts around being healthy and considering the environment.

[5] Jennifer Escalas, James Bettman. Self-Contrual, Reference Groups and Brand Meaning. 2005.

[6] I highly recommend anyone that works in an industry even tangentially connected with psychology read Kahneman's book *Thinking, Fast and Slow*. It's an incredible look at the two systems that drive the way we think: fast and slow.

[7] Numerous studies have supported these findings. Antonio Damasio, another neuroscientist, believes that emotion is a necessary part of all decisions, while Christine Born's research shows that powerful brands activate areas of the brain associated with emotion—areas that not all brands activate.

[8] You'll notice that there are differences when these phrases are translated. That's because of cultural differences related to how individual geographies relate

to their language. If you're a global business, this can be an incredibly important consideration. Even between countries that speak English as their first language there are large differences.

[9] Coke and Pepsi have long had a rivalry, being the two leading competitors in the beverage space. Over time, their language has ebbed and flowed, with a surprising lack of consistency. Just ten years earlier, in 1993, Pepsi used the slogan "Be Young, Have Fun, Drink Pepsi." While focusing on the youth market, this is much more indicative of Coke's "relax" messaging.

[10] The analysis here was conducted in mid 2019. It's likely that the language itself will change over time. However, the message should remain the same, even if you conducted the same analysis today.

Industry Semantics

[1] While organic reach and click-through had increased a year later, sales had not. This truly was a testament to the power of organic search, but it was also warning about how not to just focus on SEO and ranking. While the posts resonated with those in the community, they didn't offer a clear path to purchase or next steps. As a result, consumers would visit the pages, gain information, and then leave. As you build out content for your brand, remember that SEO is not the be all and end all of content marketing. It's only a piece of the puzzle.

In the following chapter of this book—the language of an audience—I cover what another piece of the puzzle is in detail. If I had known the second piece of the puzzle when creating a content strategy for the tech startup, I likely would have created content that resonated and was more effective.

[2] This is according to Gartner in 2019. This number has increased significantly over the years as digital practices have both afforded marketers a greater ability to make changes quickly and effectively.

[3] GAP's logo rebrand was truly one of the worst moves the company could have made. It's also a good example of what happens when data is placed above common sense. To the naked eye, GAP's revamped logo does look horrible and contradicts the brand's promise. As said by Armin Vit, designer and co-founder of UnderConsideration "Gap isn't at the frontier of fashion and its clothes are modest and safe. Consistently well-made and easy to wear. It's affordable sophistication. Their previous logo and advertising campaigns have always shared those qualities."

[4] The language of industry is really a catch-all term for the conventions and expectations set by the businesses that exist in an industry. This embodies the industry's entire approach to customers.

[5] Have these "new standards" come about because of short attention spans, or have short attention spans come about as a result of these "new standards"? The debate is still out there, with researchers from Oxford and Harvard having found a correlation between new discourse conventions on the internet and attention spans. However, correlation doesn't always mean causation.

[6] The latent semantic index (semantic keywords) is very important to ranking high in Google. It essentially

means finding words and phrases that relate to a single, core keyword, and then using them in the same piece of content. If you ever receive a piece of content from a copywriter and it only references a single keyword in their strategy, then it probably hasn't been optimized appropriately.

The Language of an Audience

[1] The Michelin brothers are credited with being two of the first marketers to implement content marketing strategies. Their Michelin Guide looked to speak to consumers not as a sales advertisement, but as a genuinely useful guidebook. The idea was that if consumers use the guidebook, they would subsequently travel further to visit these places in their cars, and so require new tires sooner.

[2] Three of those are negative emotions: sadness, fear, and anger. So it makes sense that businesses tend to project negative emotions to great effect; fear and sadness at the thought of exclusion, and anger at what is offered by competitors. But negative emotions only work so well and for a limited period of time. Consumers want to turn away from negative emotions. Fear, when used to market products, causes individuals to desperately find something to cling to; in most cases, this is a product. But what happens when that individual can replace the product with another product or another person? Fear does not encourage loyalty; it does not encourage advocates.

[3] Jonah Berger and Katherine L. Milkman. What Makes online Content Viral?

Berger and Milkman's study is interesting because it also shows that positive affect in content makes it more shareable regardless of what the content actually is. This is even if negative content is more surprising, more interesting, or more practically useful.

This almost seems counter-intuitive to what we are told about the news and media. However, think about the type of content that you share with your friends, family, and coworkers, you'll likely notice the same pattern. I, myself, often enjoy sending my wife pictures and videos of cats because I know they will make her smile.

[4] Every brand talked about on this list has a clear idea of the specific segments and audience they are targeting. This is a crucial foundation when driving Shift. If you're unsure who your audience is, it's important to engage in this research prior to beginning any research in relation to Shift.

[5] Gale and Waldron were not the first to use the specific techniques. Rather, they were two of the first to adopt them for use in marketing campaigns and for motivating advertising. While some businesses did begin to adopt these techniques early on, many took decades to adopt these practices, instead running with "gut feelings".

[6] Today, getting data like this is becoming increasingly difficult. In many cases, consumers have to opt-in to sharing their information with you. Europe has created the GDPR in order to ensure this becomes best practice. The US and other countries around the world are slowly implementing their own processes.

About the Author

Robert Bailey is a linguistic marketer that helps businesses find their language and their voice, so they can create a brand that delivers value to their customers and that resonates.

Once a dedicated academic, Robert taught linguistics and discourse analysis for three years before moving into a marketing position, and he has remained there ever since. In the last decade, Robert has worked closely with over forty brands having helped them to realize the power of their language – regardless of whether that meant creative or strategy.

A born and bred Brit living in America, when not enjoying a cup of tea you'll find him on his next great adventure – whether that's kayaking, mountain climbing, or something more esoteric.

Index

Alice in Wonderland, *83*

Alphabet, *31*

Analytics, 108, 130, 148

Android, 60

Apple
  History, *100*
  Slogan, 65
  Style, 55, *104*

Ariel, 39

Attention Span, 50, 75

Berger, Jonah, *138*

Brand
  Advocates, 45, 100, 171
  Definitions, *90*
  Guidelines, 109, 113, 125
  Loyalty, 66

Psychology, *93*

Pyramid, 58, 66

Chomsky, Noam, *27*, *86*

Christoff, Kalina, *85*

Coca Cola
  Santa Claus, 14, 37
  Vs Pepsi, *103*

Consistency
  Of a Concept, *100*

Content Farms, *116*

Content Strategy, *107*, *130*

Convenience, 60

Conventions, 11
  As Design, 16
  As Language, 20
  Social, 38

Crystal, David, *22*

Damasio, Antonio, *96*, *137*

Data
  Collection, *141*

Davis, Patrick, *90*

De Beers
  History, 20
  Pre-1947, 50
  Slogan, 53, *94*

De Saussure, Ferdinand, 32
  Signifier and Signified, 32

Decision Making
  As Emotional, 8, *96*
  As Linguistic, 10

Design
  As Language, 32
  As Timely, 43

Dove, 76

Eco, Umberto, 33

Emotion
  Happiness, *139*
  Resonance, *149*

Experiments
  Brand and Beliefs, *94*

Languages Effect on Perception, *29*

Long Shot Odds, *22*

Moral Outcomes, 10

The Gambling Task, 7

Fast Food
  As Healthy, *99*

Features vs Benefits, 61

Football, 58

Gale, Harlow, *140*

GAP, *111*

Gerace, Thomas, 50

Gerety, Frances, 20

Google
  Algorithm, *114*
  History, *113*
  Updates, *115*

Hinzen, Wolfram, *86*

HSBC, 11

Huawei
  Slogan, 64

Hypodermic Needle Model, 18

Jakobson, Roman, 34

Kahneman, Daniel, *95*

Kastner, Sabine, 75

Languages
  Latin, 4
  Mandarin, *99*
Lexicon, *102*, *162*
Linguistic Devices
  Agency, 52
  Metaphor, 6
  Omission, *87*
Linguistics
  Corpus, 78, *130*, *146*
  Dialect, 31
  Stylistics, 81
  Universal
    Grammar, *27*, *86*

Marketing
  Antiquity, 4
McDonald's
  History, 19
  I'm Lovin' It, *97*
McKee, Robert, 50
Metrics
  Awareness, *172*

Conversion, *173*
  Engagement, *171*
Michelin, *134*
Mint.com, 45
Mizen, Fred, 16
Nast, Thomas, 15, *30*
Natural Language
  Processing, *118*

New York Times, *138*
Nike
  As Potential, 48
  History, 40
  Slogan, 56
  Walt Stack, 42

Packaging, 76
Patzer, Aaron, 45
Plutchik, Robert, *137*
Psychology
  Of Uncertainty, *21*

Ringleb, Al, *21*
Rock, David, 21
Scaurus, Umbricius, 4
  Garum, 5
  Slogan, 56, *96*

Security, *132*

Segmentation, *140, 143*

Semiotics, *31*

SEO

  Citation Analysis, *115*

  Keyword Stuffing, *114*

  Keywords, *124*

  Knowledge Graph, *118*

  Latent Semantic Index, *119, 124*

  Organic Traffic, *108*

  PageRank, *114*

  Semantics, *122*

Shift

  Container, *95*

  Model, *162*

  Spectrum, 72

Sinek, Simon, 55, *101*

Slogans, 7

Social Media, *146*

Speed, 19, 61, 62

Story

  Action vs Satisfaction, 50, 57, *139*

  Elements, 51

  Protagonist, 52, 57

Stoute, Steve, *98*

Sundblom, Haddon, 15

Timberlake, Justin, *98*

Tone and Style, 54, 82

Turn-Taking, *22, 166*

User-Generated Content, *130*

Waldron, George B, *140*

Web Hosting, 61

Wheel of Emotion, *138*

Winterowd, Ross, *83*